Homemaking on the Internet

Doing up a House using the Web

Louise Hayes-Jones

Homemaking on the Internet

Doing up a House using the Web

A Dorling Kindersley book
www.dk.com

Stylist Jane Graining
Photographer Dominic Blakemore
Category Publisher Judith More
Art Director Janis Utton

Produced for Dorling Kindersley Limited by Design Revolution,
Queens Park Villa, 30 West Drive, Brighton, East Sussex, BN2 2GE
Project Editor Nicola Hodgson
Senior Designer Lucie Penn

Published in Great Britain in 2001 by Dorling Kindersley Limited,
80 Strand, London, WC2 0RL

2 4 6 8 10 9 7 5 3 1

Louise Hayes-Jones would like to acknowledge the following for their
contributions to the text: Martin Catford, Paul Jones, David Roffey and
Nick Sunderland.

A CIP catalogue record for this book is available from the British
Library

ISBN 0 7513 2164 8

Reproduced by Colourscan Overseas Co. Pte. Ltd., Singapore
Printed in Italy by L.E.G.O

Contents >>>>

Welcome to the Internet HomeMakers

We decided to bring home improvement into the technological era by broadcasting the renovation of our house live on the internet. This was just the beginning...

The family I am Louise Hayes-Jones, a fabric designer and marketeer. My husband Paul is a decorating specialist. We live in Dorset with our four children, Charlotte, Matthew, Harriet and James, whose ages range from 10 to 13, and nine Persian cats. Paul and I got engaged in 1997 and bought this bungalow together. It had been built in the 1950s, had not been decorated for more than 20 years and was in desperate need of refurbishment. Somehow we saw the potential in it, and we knew we had the skills to do a good job.

The project We made our name through launching the Internet HomeMakers website. Unique at the time, this was a live TV show broadcast over the internet that featured us refurbishing our home. We had two main motives for launching the project, one personal and one professional. I had spent six years supporting my children on Income Support before meeting Paul, and I wanted to provide security for the children. So one aim was to refurbish the house and be in a position to sell it and be able to buy another house without the bounds of a mortgage. I also wanted to use the house as a vehicle to prove my marketing skills.

The book This book is about our house, the inspiration behind its transformation, the setbacks and successes, and practical advice and hints on refurbishment, decorating and DIY. You'll be able to see how we tackled our house and hopefully be inspired to try some of the ideas and projects in your own home. It's hard work, but it's worth it to make a place your own.

▶ **Right** Paul, Harriet, Charlotte, Louise and Jamie on the front steps of Huntsmoor (Matthew was camera shy!)

The initial idea

Our first steps I had been involved in a number of internet projects prior to our establishment of the Internet HomeMakers website. My decision to go it alone was catalysed by my frustrating previous experiences in the world of business. I had found consultancies for small to medium-size businesses very discouraging because of their lack of vision and willingness to invest in their company's future. Many times I heard managing directors say 'I think we'll wait to see what our competitors do first'.

What I wanted from the internet I believe that the internet is a medium for the future, but that it has certain limitations when it comes to enterprise. For example, factors such as the speed of computers means that companies often can put only static pictures and text on their websites. I had a vision of the internet where users could visit a shop via their monitor, to be greeted by a shop assistant who would show them the goods on offer and explain all about the product as well as showing them close-ups. The ability to visit a 'live' shop would bridge the gap that internet users feel by only being able to see a static picture of a product as if it were in a catalogue. Customer and salesperson interaction would come into play and with any luck increase sales.

The internet show My original idea was to utilise live broadcasts on the internet as an educational tool for students. However, I was unable to persuade anyone else that this was feasible. My next idea was to refurbish our house on the internet using live broadcasts with webcams. I knew that many companies did not have websites and thought that the live broadcasts might show them how the internet could be used as a showcase to promote their products. At first my ideas were received with scepticism, from both friends and family and the companies I approached. However, I was positive it was going to work and I must have sounded convincing. I spent four months telephoning and visiting potential sponsors. In just one day I found more than twenty companies who were willing to donate their products to the project. The key was that I did not ask for money, only for products to refurbish our home. Many items were given at cost and some items were donated. I thought of the idea in April 1998, and we did a test broadcast in November.

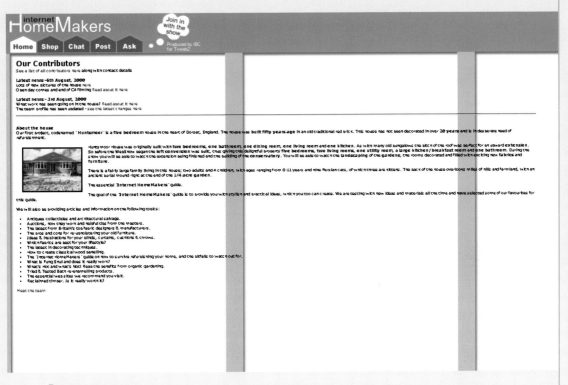

Local interest After I had recruited my sponsors and built a new website, I gave the project a launch date. Paul told me that our local news television company, Meridian, had a live news broadcast on their website. I took a look at it and emailed them to tell them what I was doing. To my surprise, they replied saying they wanted to feature our launch on their programme. After the piece was broadcast, the local newspapers contacted us, and then South West News Agency put a story together, which they subsequently sold to every national newspaper.

The escalation Everything escalated after that, and we even had news stations from France and Germany doing stories. I even did a radio interview for a station in Australia. This was in March 2000. The main refurbishment work was carried out between March and September 2000. This was quite an intense time, trying to coordinate the project, and being filmed for a documentary.

The sponsors

Finding sponsors Tracking down potential sponsors was an educational experience. First of all, I had to find the companies behind the products – I spent days in the aisles of DIY stores writing down addresses from pots and packaging. I then had to telephone the companies to find out where the head office was and try to contact the marketing department.

Convincing the sponsors My main obstacle when I was persuading sponsors to take part in the project was that there was nothing to point anyone to. There were no sites of the kind I had in mind in the USA, let alone the UK. The only live broadcasting sites that were making money were porn sites.

The sponsor experience I remember my visit to Timney Fowler very clearly. They had agreed to take part in the project and invited me to have a look at their fabrics and wallpapers. I was told I could have whatever I needed and choose the collection I liked. Being free from the restraints of a budget was a strange feeling. However, I soon pulled myself together, ignored the prices and

Below The handprinted wallpaper in the hallway by Timney Fowler

just went for something classical and smart. The Timney Fowler 'Passage in Time' collection is beautiful.

The sponsors The following companies kindly donated to the project:

- Locker and Riley supplied the ceiling mouldings
- Crown gave us all the paints we needed
- Polyvine supplied us with brushes and varnishes
- All bedroom furniture came from Laura Ashley
- Albion Bath Company supplied the bathroom suite
- Brintons Carpets supplied the carpeting
- Endon Lighting supplied the lights
- The conservatory was sponsored at cost by Portland
- The Jacuzzi was bought at cost from Certiken
- The kitchen was given at cost by Devizes Kitchens
- Neff kitchen appliances were bought at cost
- The living room sofa was supplied by Furniture Village
- The sofas in the master bedroom were sponsored by Figero Furniture
- Zoffany supplied the fabrics in the master bedroom
- The plants were bought at cost at Haskins Garden Centre
- Conservatory and garden furniture came from Habasco

▶ Top right The furniture makers Lloyd Loom made the wicker corner sofa for the conservatory. Other sofas in the house came from Furniture Village and Figero Furniture. Furniture in the conservatory, apart from the sofa, came from Habasco. They also supplied us with some garden furniture, including a pretty table and matching chairs that were ideal for outdoor dining.

Right Here you can see some of the cast iron curtain rod ends that were supplied by Clayton Munroe. They also supplied us with window latches, hinges and door handles throughout the house. I was really impressed with the quality of their goods. Also in this picture you can see some of the beautiful fabrics supplied by Zoffany. We used these in the master bedroom.

The website

Setting up the website To set the website up we teamed up with an internet provider called Keynotes. They put the pages together after we explained how we wanted them to look. It was a trial and error experience. We had nothing else to look at or use for inspiration, and it wasn't easy. We found that, because no one had done what we were doing, many of the website companies we approached did not have the experience required to broadcast live content. We faced many hurdles before getting the site up and running.

Using the webcam The webcam was an integral part of the project. I first decided to get into internet broadcasting after finding a website in 1997 that broadcast images from a webcam attached to a lamppost. This site was attracting millions of visitors. It made me realise that internet users were bored of static pages and pictures and wanted to see things or people moving in real life on their computers. There was a need to see live rather than recorded images.

Our equipment We used a basic 386 laptop back in 1998 and a four-year-old Panasonic camera. The internet company wrote some software to decode the images that were fed down the ISDN line to the internet servers. This software is available to buy, but we had to have software written specially for our requirements.

Our first broadcast From day one of the refurbishment we took pictures and kept notes of what we were doing. We did a six-week test broadcast starting in November 1998. In our first broadcasts, when we received between 5,000 and 17,000 visitors per night, we could be seen building the staircase (see p.102). The experience was very tricky. We had no training or skills as camera operators, in sound, vision or lighting. The broadcast went out between 7 and 9pm. We did this to fit in with American times in Florida as Yahoo, our internet provider, had agreed to put us on their net events pages. We asked friends to dial in and check that everything was working as the system often crashed with all the people trying to get on. Our friend Cristiana telephoned to tell us she could not see us very well, so while we were broadcasting Paul rushed out to buy some halogen lights.

Coping without sound Our technology was quite basic in the early days of the website, and we didn't have the facility to put sound out. My dad, who was helping Paul to renovate the staircase, would stand in front of the camera and tell the world what he was doing, just like a proper television presenter. It took a few days for him to realise that internet viewers couldn't hear us! We bought writing boards to hold up in front of the camera to explain what was going on. We had to write in large letters on the board, which meant that we could not get all the message on the computer screen and had to broadcast sentences in two halves. Anyone visiting us when we were sending out the second part must have wondered what was going on. It was very funny. The other problem was that the image would change every ten seconds. First you'd see me, then I'd be gone – brilliant for magic tricks! Most of our visitors in the test project back in 1998 were American, but within six weeks I had discovered countries I had never heard of.

How the website evolved We gradually had more people involved with the refurbishment of the house and the garden, and they featured on the website broadcasts too. For example, Martin Catford, who landscaped our garden, did broadcasts about the garden design and the materials we used.

Below A sample page from our website

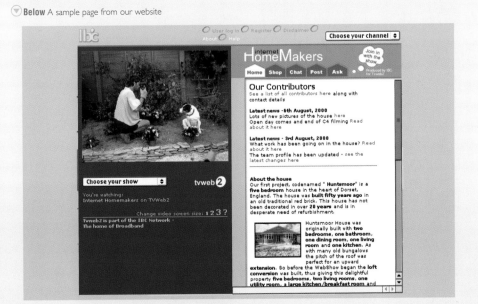

Setting up your own website

Getting started You may want to set up your own internet broadcasting site. You could keep a record of the refurbishment of your own house. Or you could use it as a way of keeping in touch with relatives in distant countries, perhaps videoing and broadcasting family parties. It isn't particularly complicated to set up. The main pieces of equipment that you need are a video capture card and a video encoding program. You also need a fast internet connection.

Video encoding programs The two main types of encoders available are Microsoft Media Encoder, which is available free, or Real Media's RealProducer, which costs about £200. There may be other programs available, but the two mentioned above are the most widely used. If software is popular then it is likely that your visitors will be able to see what you are doing straight away. If they do not have any of the above software already downloaded, they will need to obtain it before being able to watch the live images. If you use a different kind of software to capture your live images then make sure you include a version to download on your website. Future developments in

Below Louise filming Paul on the webcam

software encoders will allow the software to recognise a digital video stream. This means that cameras and laptops that can communicate via Firewire or IEEE1394, such as the Sony Vaio laptops and Sony digital camcorders, will be a perfect solution for the home broadcaster.

Video capture cards A desktop computer will give the most flexibility in the types of video capture card that you can use. Leaders in the field are the cards from Osprey and Pinnacle Systems. You can use a laptop, but only if you have a powerful one that has a USB port. You will also need a capture device with a laptop as you cannot use standard video capture cards with one. The USB port is the only one fast enough to do a decent job on a laptop. The best device for price and performance currently available is one from Belkin called the 'Videobus'.

Internet connection You will need a fast connection to the internet. An ISDN (integrated services digital network) line is ideal, but you can achieve limited success with a good modem connection. You can get an even better connection to the internet with ADSL (asynchronous digital subscriber line), cable or leased lines. All the time that you are broadcasting you will be racking up call charges. You will also need an ISP (internet service provider) that supports video streaming – some support Realproducer and some support Media Encoder. Some support both, but these are harder to find. If you are using Media Encoder you will need to find an ISP that offers a fixed IP (internet protocol – i.e. a unique address) for dial-ups as this is a requirement for broadcasting.

Bandwidth costs The main problem with broadcasting is bandwidth costs – if you are broadcasting at low quality then bandwidth costs currently work out at around £15 per simultaneous viewer. Economies of scale mean that this cost can drop to a much lower figure, but only if you are attracting thousands of simultaneous viewers. Some ISPs will offer up to 100 simultaneous streams as part of their package – do some research and shop around to find the best deals available before you commit.

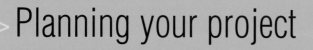

Planning your project

Here you can see the room layouts for the ground floor of the bungalow before we did any work to it. (Measurements are given in metres.)

- My strongest impression when walking around the house for the first time was the darkness of the hallway and the kitchen. The kitchen was tiled in a dull green, which made the room seem even darker. Then there was the dull wallpaper and the dull carpets. In fact, everything was going against it, and it was difficult to see beyond these things.

- I noticed the bathroom toilet as I walked down the hallway. The door hung in such a way that if anyone did not close the door properly you had an unsightly view of the toilet. If ever I was caught off-guard by an unexpected visitor, I would find myself running one step ahead of them to close the toilet lid and shut the bathroom door. This was really irritating!

- The living room felt awkward, as you had to cross the hallway from the kitchen and walk through the lounge to sit in the dining room. It is better either to have a dining room off your kitchen or have a separate room that can be left and the dirty dishes not seen once you have moved to the lounge area.

- The third bedroom was badly placed, too. I believe it was meant to be a dining room as it had sliding doors to the back garden. I do not think the builder intended this room for a bedroom, because no one sleeping in here would be happy about people walking through their room to the back garden whenever they chose. I imagine the house was a two-bedroom house at its conception.

- I hated all the secondary glazing. I like to keep things as clean as possible, and the way secondary glazing is attached to the inside of your current window, it leaves a gap for flies to die and dry up in. This means you need to remove the whole system to give it a really healthy clean.

Symbols

 Feng Shui Tips on Feng Shui from our consultant

 DIY tips How to do the job like the professionals

 Life tips How to keep you and your family happy

 Timetable tips Advice on timetabling and keeping to schedule

 Planning tips Advice on how to plan the work

 Diary The inside story on what we did and why

 Internet tips Useful websites, using the internet

 Warning Common mistakes and possible dangers to avoid

 Timesavers Handy tips to save time and cut corners

 Moneysavers Tips on budgeting and getting value for money

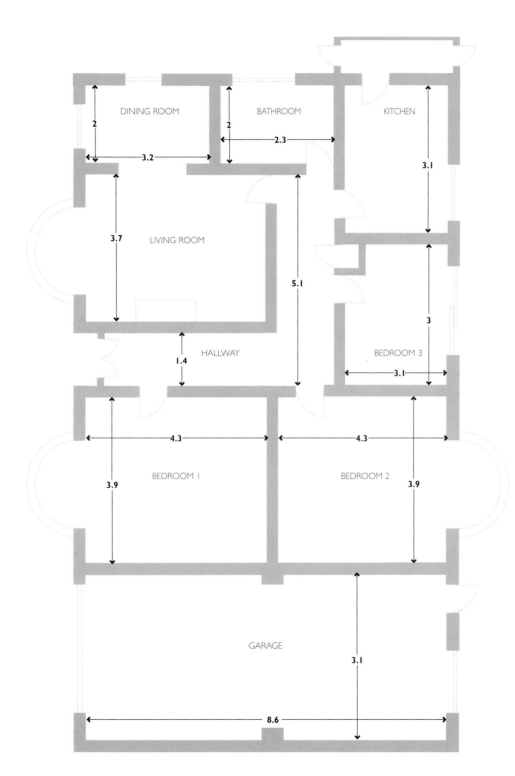

DINING ROOM

2

3.2

BATHROOM

2

2.3

KITCHEN

3.1

3.7

LIVING ROOM

5.1

3

HALLWAY

1.4

BEDROOM 3

3.1

4.3

4.3

BEDROOM 1

3.9

BEDROOM 2

3.9

GARAGE

3.1

8.6

Measurements in metres

This plan shows the ground floor after our remodelling and refurbishment. We have organised the rooms to suit the light.

- The kitchen is now one-third larger, and we have created a new utility room. This is an area we keep coats, shoes and outdoor items in, and where we feed the cats. It's also really useful for containing any mess from the children in one small area.

- The former living room is now a bedroom. However, it could equally well be used as a living room again, as the double doors leading out on to the timber decking outside make this room quite versatile. I was originally going to make this en suite area into a bathroom. However, this would have meant that this room would always have to be used as a bedroom, and I wanted the option to use this room as a living room when I have a furniture move-around. When the children are older this would be very useful for them as a living room.

- We converted one of the bedrooms into a living room and extended it via the old garage, which is now a conservatory.

- The conservatory has a doorway to the back garden, and has wonderful views over the garden, including the water feature, the rock garden and the open fields beyond.

- The stairway to the loft conversion is the first thing that you notice as you enter the house. Because of this, I wanted to create impact in the hallway, which is why I chose to fit an old, renovated staircase.

- The hallway is where the first impressions of your home are made, and is the taster that makes your guest wonder what the rest of the house is like.

Expert advice

 Diary

The best property for you may not be the obvious one. I did not much like the bungalow when I first saw it. I had imagined living in an old town house with high ceilings. However, my ideal inspired me to design the bungalow to feel like a country home. The bungalow had three bedrooms, including one that you could walk through to the big back garden, which was basically no more than a pony paddock. However, somehow we managed to see the potential in it and could envisage turning it into our dream home by extending into the loft and garage to provide four bedrooms and more living accommodation.

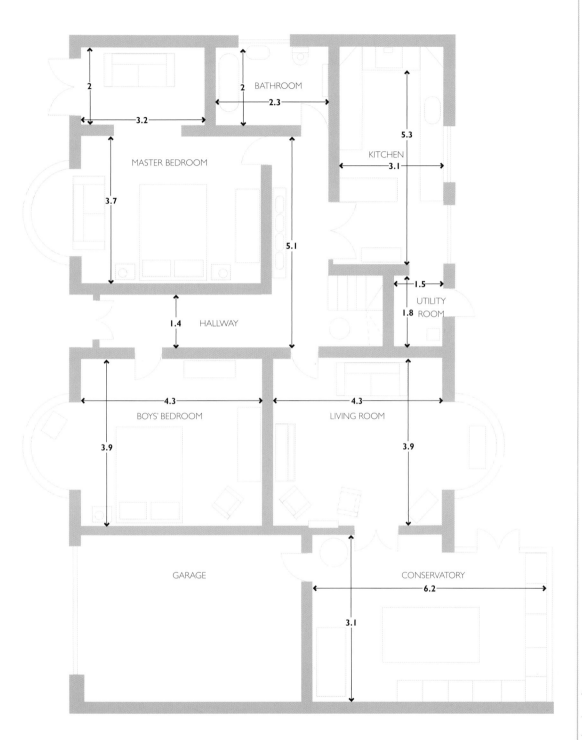

MASTER BEDROOM

BATHROOM

2

2

2.3

3.2

3.7

KITCHEN

5.3

3.1

5.1

1.5

1.8

UTILITY
ROOM

1.4

HALLWAY

BOYS' BEDROOM

LIVING ROOM

4.3

4.3

3.9

3.9

GARAGE

CONSERVATORY

6.2

3.1

Measurements in metres

This loft conversion meant freedom for many in this family. The ability for us to expand our living space into the loft area was one of the reasons why we bought this bungalow in the first place. We desperately needed the extra space for bedrooms for the children. We also intended to create a second bathroom up there, because with six people in the household, our small downstairs bathroom is in heavy use.

We had lived in the bungalow for a year before starting the loft conversion. By then the children were really needing their own space, because they had all grown so much that the house was beginning to feel much too cramped. All the children were sharing one room, which wasn't a good situation. There were lots of squabbles breaking out between them. The loft conversion was brilliant. There was a real sense of achievement watching the transformation by fitting the largest window we could find, and then observing the rooms take shape. When the rooms were built, we still had another six months before the lighting was wired. We also had no staircase, and had to go up and down by a stepladder.

- Harriet and Charlotte have their own bedrooms.

- We intended two of these rooms to be used as bedrooms for the boys, although at the moment they are happier in one of the downstairs bedrooms.

- I use one room as my study. The other room we currently use as a storeroom, although it offers the potential to be converted into an extra bathroom, which would be useful in a family of our size.

- We did not allow for too much hall space as it is not necessary. Additional room space was our priority and as long as you do not bump noses when you leave your rooms, it is perfectly ample.

Expert advice

 Diary

When we first looked at the house, Paul says that the immediate thing that I noticed was that the garden was big enough for a marquee for our wedding reception. Obviously my main consideration should have been the state of the house and the size of the rooms. Eventually I got my priorities sorted and focused on the house rather than the garden. The house was very out of date, but as we looked around Paul and I were discussing all the things that we could change. The list of things that we wanted to do was very long, and when we moved in we both felt pretty overwhelmed.

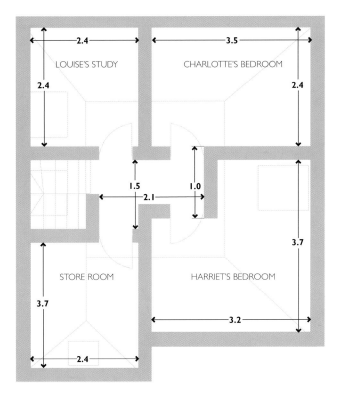

LOUISE'S STUDY

2.4

2.4

CHARLOTTE'S BEDROOM

3.5

2.4

1.5

1.0

2.1

STORE ROOM

3.7

2.4

HARRIET'S BEDROOM

3.7

3.2

Measurements in metres

Finding the house

Setting your criteria When you are looking for a house you need to set a list of criteria. Like many parents, we chose the area first because of the school we wanted to get the children into, which has an outstanding reputation. After looking for a while and not being able to agree on anything, Paul and I evolved a stringent checklist to sort out our main priorities. This included the number of bedrooms – there are six of us in our family, so we needed an absolute minimum of three bedrooms. Luckily, the children's ages are close together so at least they could share rooms for a while, but we also had to think to the future because they would eventually require their own rooms. This meant that another priority was buying a property that we could extend.

The choice we made The bungalow we eventually decided on buying met most of the criteria on our checklist. It was near a primary school with an excellent reputation. It had two bedrooms and a dining room that was being used as a third bedroom. It also offered the scope to build up, by converting the loft, or on, by building an extension. The house was also near to a regular bus route into the local town. It had a large enclosed garden for the children to play safely and was big enough to hold the marquee for our wedding reception – a major concern at the time!

Starting the hunt Start by looking in the property papers. They will give you an idea of what is available in the immediate locality and the surrounding areas in terms of price ranges and styles of homes. However, this is just a starting point. No estate agent lists all the properties that they have for offer. If you have internet access, this can prove very useful and is also a real time-saver. Estate agents with websites can list all of their properties complete with pictures, so you can browse hundreds of properties, 24 hours a day, without having to go to the agents to pick up details. We also drove around the area we wanted to move to looking for 'for sale' signs. That is how we found our property.

Expert advice

 Moneysavers

It's worth noting that family houses tend to hold their value in an area where there is a good school.

 Diary

Paul left me to do most of the leg work in the days before we had internet access. For a couple of months all we seemed to do was go out and look at properties. It became very tiresome, especially as we could never agree on what we liked. Be warned, searching for a home is a long and tedious process that puts stress on the most loving of relationships.

Keep your vision Buying a house that needs a lot of attention and refurbishment is a challenge. Bear this in mind when you are looking for a home. If you are easily discouraged and feel that you do not have the skills, commitment and stamina to do extensive improvement and remodelling work, you should perhaps choose a house that is in a better condition. It can be dispiriting. When we first moved to our new home, the bathroom was so grotty it made us want to bathe only at the local swimming pool, and the kitchen facilities were such that we frequently resorted to takeaways. I cried the first night, not so much for joy at owning my first home but at the realisation of the immense task that lay before us. However, what kept us going was our mission to alter and adapt the house so that we could justifiably call it our home. I suspect the previous owners of our house might well recognise the outline of what was once their home, but not much else.

Left Our bungalow after the refurbishment. We drew up a strict list of criteria when we were looking for our property, and this is the key to finding a home that you'll be happy in.

Expert advice

 Diary

When we looked for the house originally, we had a time limit, as we were getting married on the August bank holiday and wanted to be in and settled so we could organise the wedding reception. Be aware that completing a sale often takes longer than expected. As it was, we moved in eight weeks before the wedding.

 Moneysavers

Think about how you could increase your property's value by adding on extras such as a new kitchen, bathroom, conservatory, extension or loft conversion.

Buying a house: questions and answers

Q **What are some useful criteria when deciding what to look for in a property?**

A Ask yourself what you need from your prospective home. Are there adequate bathroom facilities or will people be queuing to get in for a wash in the morning? Can everyone eat in the kitchen, or where else will meals be consumed? Is it possible for everyone to have their own room or a spare room for guests? Is there space to have a room for hobbies or a room for the children to keep their toys? Do you need a quiet room where the adults can escape to read a book or newspaper or have a conversation? Do you need room for a home office? More and more people are working from home, and this was an issue for us. We had to provide a place that would enable Louise to be able to concentrate on her work away from the home environment – i.e. the kids and the cats! You also need to look at access to the property. It is as important getting around your property as it is getting in and out. Is it possible to access the rear of the property without coming through the house? And consider whether you have enough room to park your vehicles within your boundary. Think about security issues, too – for example, are the walls or fences adequate to deter burglars?

Q **What factors are important when choosing an area to live in?**

A The area that your house is in may influence the value of your house. Having a reputable school in the area will definitely add value. Other factors that may have an impact include whether the house is near a main road; whether it is close to towns; whether there is convenient access to shops and other facilities; and whether it is near a road that is a 'rat run', (a short cut to work for people in the morning). Try to find out what plans there are for road developments over the next five years. You can check for possible planning developments yourself because they are matters of public record. It's also worth knocking on the neighbours' doors for a social chat. You can ask questions about the area, as well as seeing whether you want to live next to those people!

Q **I'm going to have a survey done, but is there anything I can look for myself?**

A It's very important to have a survey done. However, not all surveyors are aware of conservation issues, so make sure that you find one who is. A survey that will provide you with conservation knowledge and defects advice will cost around £400, and that does not include your valuation survey. Make sure that you have a detailed account of what you are paying for, i.e. check that the cost of a conservation expert's advice is included in the surveyor's fees. However, there are a couple of things you can look out for yourself on older properties. One is to look out for cracks in the rendering, especially in thatched properties. These tend to have walls rendered in original material that contains lime, which is relatively weak. For a number of years, some thatches have had their renders repaired with cement, which is not a suitable material. Cement is usually stronger than the original rendering, and can shrink against and move away from it. This can explain why you may hear a tapping noise when you tap the outside render. A lot of Victorian properties have a problem with corrosion of the wall ties in the cavity. Sometimes it is necessary to have a section of cavity ties exposed to look for any corrosion.

Q **What things are important to look out for in a garden?**

A You should check what direction your garden faces. This has a bearing on where you can plant sun- or shade-loving plants. If you like to laze in your garden and to entertain guests, you can work out the best areas to sunbathe in or to place your garden furniture. Also check where the prevailing winds are, as these have a bearing on which plants you can cultivate.

Q Is it important to find out what type of land my house is built on?

A It is a good idea to find out what the land was used for before it was built on. If the land was waste land or used for a dump, this could cause problems. Housing estates built over waste disposal areas often have problems because drainage and water pipes erode quickly. There was also a case where houses were built on clay before a particularly hot summer in the 1970s. Some houses that were built before that year have suffered from land subsidence. The clay dried up so much that the footings moved underneath the houses and many of them required underpinning, which is a very expensive rescue operation.

Q What considerations are there when restoring an old property?

A One important consideration is that the property may be a listed building. This has implications when it comes to restoration, as listed buildings have specific guidelines on what materials you are allowed to use in the refurbishment process. Old building materials, such as bricks, tend to be rare and therefore expensive. Trying to track down adequate quantities of materials can also be time-consuming and difficult.

Q What's the first thing to do when planning a refurbishment?

A The first thing you must do is check your building insurance. You may not be covered for making alterations on your home and you may need to make adjustments to your policy. Also bear in mind that as you increase the size and value of your property your policy will not cover the changes. Try to get advice from a surveyor or estate agent as to the value you will be adding to your property. This will fluctuate according to the state of the property market, so keep your eye on this issue.

Q How do you go about planning and arranging loft conversions?

A If you are thinking about building an extension in your roof space, you need to have an architect check it over. The roof structure has to be able to take the weight of a new floor, which means that the roof timbers may need reinforcing. The roof height also may be too low, as there is a required minimum height in the building regulations.

Q Is there a limit to how much money you should put into refurbishment?

A A house will generally have a maximum value on the market whatever improvements you make to it and no matter how you decorate it. Talk to your estate agent about your plans and ask for advice on what the value of your property may be when you have completed your work. This will give you an indication of when you should stop spending, or even how much it is worth doing to your home in the first place.

Q What factors should be taken into account when planning extensions?

A People often think about building an extension to their house and don't really think about the best place for it or how they are going to put their new space to best use. For example, in our house an extension had been built by the previous owners from the living room (see plan on page 19) to be used as a dining room. The extension was divided from the original part of the bungalow by an archway. This meant it was difficult to put chairs against the wall and see people in the main lounge area. It was also pointless as a dining area as the kitchen was on the other side of the hall. We turned the living room into a bedroom and the dining room into a sitting area, giving the extension a more practical purpose. We built decking outside the sitting area, which extended the room even more and increased its versatility.

Finding the team

Our team Paul and I had a distinct advantage when it came to the refurbishment of our house as we both work in the trade. Paul has always lived in the area and is a well respected decorator. Therefore he was in constant contact with other tradespeople such as plumbers and electricians. Interior design was something I had a flair for, and I knew all I needed to about fabrics. This made the project cost-effective as Paul's and my time was free. The rest of the team did not come together until January 2000, except for Nick Sunderland, the Feng Shui consultant (see p.154), who had been involved since November 1998, and gardener Martin Catford, who came on board in April 1999.

The evolution of the team I did not recruit the whole team at once as we did not know when we would be ready for the different tradespeople to work on the project. However, we recruited through word-of-mouth recommendations, and we found people who would keep a gap in their schedule. This is often a

 Right Martin Giles is a builder and landscaper who has been involved in many heritage restoration projects. He built the water feature in the garden with guidance from Martin Catford.

Expert advice

 Diary
Our electrician, David Watts, did all the rewiring on our house, most importantly in the bathroom, where we had had to cope with only having candlelight for

nearly a year. We also had the joy of having hot water at last and not having to walk down the road to a friend's house to have a bath!

Planning tips
If you can't find someone via a recommendation, try directories like the Yellow Pages, the listings in local papers or adverts in specialist magazines. But make sure the person is insured, and get a detailed quotation for the work.

problem when you are trying to plan a project – skilled, trustworthy tradespeople tend to get booked up. However, it is worth holding out for someone reliable than hiring someone who is available at short notice but who does a poor job.

Finding reliable tradespeople If you need a builder to do any work on your property, before taking them on you can check with a number of builders' associations who will be able to advise you whether your builder is on their records. It's possible that a disreputable builder may have been struck off their records. Never take anything on trust. As an added precaution, ask your builder for their certificate of insurance. This protects them should they damage your property. Do not be afraid to ask for a copy and check out any liability clauses they are not covered for. Remember, if anything happens and they are not covered, you will not receive any compensation. If the builder does not have sufficient money to repair the damage then all you can do is to make sure they do not work as a builder again. It is in your best interests to check these things out beforehand.

Recommendations Don't underestimate word of mouth. This is one of the most common methods of finding people who will do a good job, and it is often effective. However, it is still worthwhile checking that the person recommended to you is registered and insured. The best people to give you recommendations are insiders – think of someone you know and trust in the building trade, whether it is a plumber, carpenter or builder. They will have numerous trustworthy and capable contacts they can put you in touch with. This is what we did. Through his work, Paul knew good plumbers and general builders, and in turn they recommended people that they were confident would do quality work.

Above Martin Catford, our landscape gardener. Martin was responsible for realising our rough ideas for the complete redesign of the garden.

Above left Steve Dalison, our landscaper and bricklayer. He constructed our dry stone walls and also built the new brick walls for the conservatory.

Planning and preparation

Above A large part of planning your project will consist of trying to find appropriate materials. In our case, we wanted to use a lot of salvaged items and restore them, so our planning process included plenty of visits to antique shops, salvage and reclamation yards, local dumps and car boot sales.

My guidelines The main thing to bear in mind when planning a project and choosing designs is to reflect your own personality, interests and tastes. There is no point designing a home and spending lots of money if you are not reflecting your individuality. You will just spend the next few years buying extras that don't match, or make each room an awkward jumble of styles. Each room in my home has a purpose for me and my family. It helps us feel good when we are with each other and helps us feel relaxed with guests. If you decorate your home for you it will help you feel relaxed, inspired and confident.

Making plans A useful tip for making plans is to create a project folder for each room. Our folder consisted of:

- brochures from sponsors about the products that were going into the room
- a room layout
- list of jobs to do that we ticked off as we went along
- invoices and receipts
- a picture board with cuttings of fabric, dabs of paint colour and any pictures of products.

Getting inspiration You can use these folders initially for things that inspire you for decorating themes. You can put in cuttings from magazines, paint charts, samples of fabrics, samples of different wallpapers, tiling and flooring catalogues and pictures of furniture. There are many different magazines on interiors and decorating on the market, so whether your tastes are for urban minimalism or for something more traditional, you'll find something to inspire you. You can also include in the project folders items such as plans and measurements for the room and contact details of contractors and suppliers.

Using the folders Our folders were designed so that everyone involved in the project could get access to the information we held for each room. For

Expert advice

 Diary

It's usually sensible to do one room at a time. However, in our case each room needed gutting, ceilings plastering, and floors sanding, so we worked through each room tackling the messy jobs first.

 DIY tips

When painting ceilings, wear a peaked baseball-style cap to prevent paint getting in your eyes or hair – rollers tend to flick dots of paint around.

 Details

I discovered some time ago that engine cleaner is excellent for bringing out wooden floors.

example, if David, our electrician, wanted to know which lights were being used, he had only to look in the files. You can also use them to keep track of the financial side of things, for example, your original budgeting and costings for the job along with quotations, estimates and invoices from suppliers and tradespeople. Once you have completed a room, you can use the project folder to keep a record of the names, codes and manufacturer's reference of any products that you have used, for example, if you need to order another roll of matching wallpaper or to touch up a paint job.

The first spree Many people when they first move into the house want to remove traces of the previous inhabitants as soon as they can in order to put their own mark on the place and make it feel like their own home. However, if you can bear to wait, it's a good idea to live in your home for a year before deciding how to decorate so you can experience the house through the four seasons. You can observe how the light works in each room, whether a room gets the sun in the morning or afternoon, whether rooms are draughty or stuffy, whether they would work better with warmer or cooler colours. A spacious room in white and cool blues may be appealing on hot summer days, but may feel offputtingly chilly in the middle of a wet winter.

Above Some of the reclaimed wooden floorboards that we decided to put down throughout the house.

What we did Waiting for a year before you decorate does not mean that you have to live with peeling wallpaper, chipped paintwork and old carpets that you hate, however. In the first few weeks of living in the house, we had an initial decorating spree in which we stripped wallpaper, ripped up carpets, put down laminate flooring and painted all the walls and ceilings white. This was to create a blank canvas before deciding what theme to create in each room. After we'd lived there for a year, we converted the loft. We made four rooms up there, two bedrooms for the girls, an office, and a store room. Then we were ready to tackle the ground floor.

Timetabling

Right One thing you can be sure of is that your project will be delayed because of unforeseen circumstances! In this instance, a crowd of curious cows hindered us as we dismantled the fence at the end of the garden.

Timetabling the work It's a good idea to draw up a rough timetable for your work, particularly if you have extensive refurbishment to do, as we did. This helps when you are budgeting and enables you to organise everything, for example, making sure you have the materials you need, and can pay for them, when you are ready to tackle that particular job.

The main phases There are four main phases to go through when you refurbish your property:

• Phase one is tackling the major building and preparation work. This includes anything messy such as replastering walls and ceilings, demolition works such as knocking down internal walls, replacing floors or sanding down wooden floors. This stage also includes the fixing of new doorways and hanging new doors, and the installation of new windows.

• Phase two is the replacement stage. This includes ripping out old fixtures and fitting new bathroom suites, kitchen units, panelling, ceiling mouldings and fireplaces.

Expert advice

 Life tips

• If you have children, resign yourself to the fact you may never finish decorating because you will be cleaning and repainting as dust and muck get trodden around the home!

• We had an artificial deadline set because of filming the television documentary. In normal circumstances you will do each stage as and when you can. If you stay in phase one for too long you will become frustrated and disheartened. It is not good to live in a bomb site for too long, nor is it healthy.

- Phase three is the decorating stage, including painting walls and ceilings, wallpapering, the fixing of light fittings and staining and varnishing floors or laying down carpets.
- Phase four consists of placing the furniture and adding finishing touches such as curtains, cushions and rugs.

What we did first In the first few months we removed the secondary glazing on windows and stripped all the paint off the windows on the inside to take them back to the original timber. We also fitted traditional leaded glass into the windows. We then had a six-month lull as I was unemployed and we couldn't afford to do any work on the house. Then in March 1998 we converted the loft – the children had all been sleeping in one room and we needed to give them more space. Between April and November I was setting up the trial internet project and getting sponsors. In November 1998 we fitted the staircase up to the loft. From January to August 2000 the main work was completed, although in August 1999 we fitted the timber decking outside.

Our order of work I spent two months costing the project and creating room plans with fabric boards and furniture layouts on paper. We tackled messy jobs throughout the house such as plastering, repairing floors and sanding down the wooden floors. We then started work on the rooms, which we did in the following order:
- the boys' bedroom
- the bathroom
- the master bedroom and its adjoining living room
- the conservatory
- the kitchen
- the hallway
- the main living room
- Harriet's bedroom

The other rooms in the loft conversion were to be done at a later stage.

Keeping the project on track It took us about six months to complete phase one of the project. While we were working on the later rooms, including the conservatory and the kitchen, during the summer, tons of boulders, stone chippings, turf, gravel and plants were being delivered for the transformation of the garden. I had to check constantly that all the people involved in the project had the resources and materials that they needed. I also had to make sure that materials were delivered on time so the team were never held up. Be warned – you need to be organised!

Below The delivery of the materials you need must be carefully coordinated. In our case it was quite a task because of the large quantities that were involved.

Bottom We demolished part of the old garage to make way for the new conservatory. Messy work such as knocking down walls should be undertaken in the first phase of refurbishment work.

Budgeting

Trying to budget Budgeting is often a difficult task. People are rarely in the fortunate situation where they have enough money to do all their refurbishment in one sweep. Most people do the work as and when they have the money. For example, I lost my job shortly after we moved in, which meant that we could do no work for six months as we had only one wage to live on.

Working out costs Once we had won sponsorship via the internet, it meant that we did not have to budget for the refurbishment of the house in the usual way. However, in normal circumstances, you should list everything that needs to be done for each room and for the outside of the house. Find out what the costs are for doing any work such as replastering and for materials such as wallpaper and paints. When it comes to making a budget for paints, fabrics, furniture, fixtures and fittings, there are always expensive products and cheaper alternatives. If you see your ideal fabric but it is more expensive than you can afford, look for similar alternatives. For example, we used Clayton Munroe's fixtures and fittings. The curtain rods and curtain ends are solid metal and of outstanding quality. But there are alternatives made of plastic that are much cheaper. You will have to leave budgets for cosmetic items till last if you have building works to do.

Budgeting for materials Building and DIY materials can vary a lot in their price and quality, but it is a general rule that you get what you pay for. It's often worth going for more expensive items because the overall effect not only looks better but lasts longer. For example, good quality paint may be more expensive, but you will need fewer coats, while better quality flooring will last longer.

Buying salvaged items I'm a great believer in bargain-hunting, and many of the items in our house were salvaged from dumps, car boot sales and reclamation yards. Some people do not have the time or energy to dispose of unwanted

Expert advice

Moneysavers

We found two reclaimed 300-year-old wooden beams for our kitchen. If you are looking at beams, check them out for dry rot and woodworm. You can do a basic prod test on areas that look dubious. Soft, crumbly areas will have to be scraped away, so check how deep the

softness or dry areas go. There are some good treatments for woodworm if your beam has any, and some excellent dry rot treatment that hardens the timber. The beams we chose had a little dry rot, but it was just enough to add character rather than gaping holes.

Details

If you can't afford an expensive reproduction bathroom suite, look for an original. If you buy one in less than pristine condition, it is possible to buy good re-enamelling kits to restore it. The new enamel may last up to five years.

items by selling them, so just take them to the dump. I have found fantastic pieces at such places — old silk rugs, antique chairs, Cornish ware, period fabrics (which are very collectable), and picture frames. Spring is a good time to visit such places as this is often a time when people have a clearout of their attics and garages, and their rubbish could be your treasure. Be disciplined, however. If you are looking for an item of furniture, take measurements of the area you are trying to fill before you start your salvage hunt. Many salvaged items have to be restored in some way. If you don't have time to do that job yourself or would rather trust it to an expert, get a quotation for the work. If you are buying building materials such as bricks, check the availability if you run out and need to buy more. It's a costly mistake if you build half a wall and run out of bricks.

Bargain hunting To be able to buy real bargains you need cash set aside especially for when you see something you need. If you aren't strict with yourself you can be sure that when the bargains come up you won't have the money. Be aware that bargains are not always found in the sales. Some people buy an item purely because it is reduced and feel proud of their saving, whether they wanted that item or not. If you don't need the object, it's not a bargain! For example, if I had not found the shop counter that we use as a breakfast bar in the kitchen, I would have left the space empty until I found the right item. Try to avoid buying an item as a temporary measure because you are likely to be unhappy with it and invariably end up wasting your money because you will eventually replace it.

Hidden costs You also need to take into account hidden costs. For example, when you remove a wall you may accidentally damage another wall by removing a brick that pulls plaster off a wall that is sound. Things like this are money losers, and are often why jobs take longer and cost more than people expect. If you pay someone to do the whole job for you make sure you get an itemised quotation detailing what you are paying for.

Buying on the internet A lot of people seem to be wary about using the internet for financial transactions. I think that there has been a lot of scaremongering in the press about the safety of buying on the web. I believe this has been done to try to stop buyers moving sales away from conventional suppliers. Perhaps big companies are frightened by the potential that the internet offers consumers to buy products and cut costs. The internet has also allowed internet companies to develop more quickly than conventional stores.

Internet safety I believe that buying over the internet is the safest way to use your credit card, far safer than booking cinema tickets over the telephone or handing your card to a waiter when you pay a bill in a restaurant. The waiter could write down your card number on the payment slip, for example. I buy a

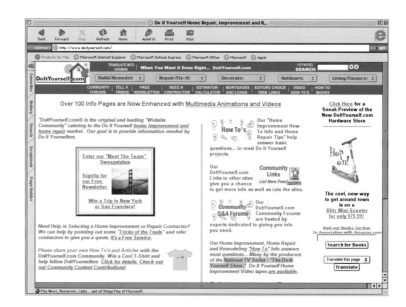

Right It is possible to find internet sites giving you advice on DIY and decorating. This is a good place to start if you are going to tackle a job that you have no previous experience of.

Internet tips

- www.which.net/webtrader is a list of internet shopping sites that meet the standards of the UK's Consumer Association.

- I-Escrow.com is an organisation that deals with secure internet transactions. The site acts as a go-between between vendors and purchasers.

- www.traderlist.com is a useful site that contains a database of both bad and recommended traders.

lot of my goods via the internet now, and often at a fraction of the cost of buying from a conventional supplier in the UK. If you are thinking of doing this, check the company's return policy. You can try emailing them to find out how long they have been around if you want further reassurance. In addition, some laws have been introduced to monitor buying on the web, so don't be scared and see what bargains you can find.

Safety measures If you are thinking of buying something over the internet and want to check the security of the site before you give out personal financial details, there are a number of checks that you can make. Look to see whether the website address starts with the prefix 'https' rather than the standard http. The 's' stands for 'secure' (and the http, for what it's worth, stands for 'hyper text transfer protocol'.) This means that when you send your financial details to the site, it is sent in an encrypted form.

Monitoring and certification In recognition that many consumers are wary of shopping over the internet, there are now a number of ombudsman-type internet authorities that monitor the security of vendor sites. For example, there is one in the USA that is overseen by the government. In the UK, the Consumer Association puts its seal of approval on internet shopping sites that agree to uphold its rigorous trading standards.

Bargains and discounts The internet is a good source to find items at a better price than you might obtain elsewhere. There are several reasons for this; one is that there are thousands of sites competing for potentially millions of customers worldwide, so their prices need to be keen. There are also sites that monitor vendor sites and compare prices. If there is something specific that you want, you can log on and find out which site offers the best deal. There are also a number of auction sites where you can bid for what you want.

Below Many suppliers and manufacturers have set up internet sites to advertise and sell their products. Even if you don't want to buy these items, these websites are a good place to visit for inspiration.

Keeping your family happy

The stresses in our family Buying this house and refurbishing it created a lot of stress for us. Paul and I bought the house two months before we got married, and we did not take into account the strain of arranging a wedding, or the emotional turmoil the kids would be put under settling into new schools. Then came the stress caused by the refurbishment; for example, having to drive eight miles after work to the swimming baths because we couldn't use the bathroom. Paul and I became tired and grouchy, and the kids followed suit. The kitchen was dismantled not long after the bathroom was stripped out so we had nowhere to eat together either. When we were being filmed for the documentary, the camera crew had us hooked up to microphones all day, and these picked up every outburst of temper. Paul and I avoided each other so that we would not say what we really thought of each other on camera.

Turning the situation around Eventually, our family became fragmented for too long. We had put ourselves under so much pressure that we went into survival mode and stopped communicating with each other. When we reached our lowest point, I moved into a caravan in the front garden with the kids. Spending time with the children is what really turned the situation around. I realised that they were really suffering from all the disruption and not having a regular routine. Gathering round the portable television in the caravan gave the children somewhere to hide from all the commotion and just relax together. Mobile homes are quite cheap to hire, and anyone embarking on what we did would be well advised to consider doing this from the start.

Drawing up rotas It is a good idea to draw up a rota for the family. You will save yourself a lot of pressure if everyone knows when to have their dirty washing ready, who is responsible for what chores and when they do them, which day you do grocery shopping, or which day to spend together as a family. It may be difficult to keep to the rota at first, but after a couple of weeks it will become

Below The children were keen to try out the Jacuzzi as soon as it was installed!

Expert advice

Diary

Be prepared for the fact that arguments will flare up and stresses will be placed on even the strongest of relationships. It is important to be clear about who is going to tackle each task, and agree the division of labour. Paul and I had a falling-out over the digger that we hired for the garden. I had started using it because we were so short of time. It took me a while to get the hang of it, and Paul told me off and gave me a lecture on how to do it properly. He wanted to use it himself and I was made to ride the dumper truck. By the end of the day we were no longer talking and I think we ignored each other for a day or two after.

planning your project

habit. It's wise to get the routines in order before chaos sets in, not when it's nearly too late like we did.

Above Harriet and Charlotte busy painting the garden fence. If there are any safe and simple jobs you can give to your children, they will enjoy being involved and feeling important.

Maintaining communication It's important to keep channels of communication open. You should spend time with your family at least one day a week so you are in touch with what is happening in their lives and they will understand you a little better too. Make it the same day every week, as children thrive on consistency. Even when you are not working on the house it can be depressing to sit and look at all the chaos and think about all the work that needs to be done. We made a point of leaving the house to go on a trip together on our family days. These days really helped us to keep going, and it was a relief to take a break from all the mess.

Pressures on relationships This project put a lot of stress on my marriage. Things got so bad that Paul and I were planning to divorce each other once the house was sold. The project played a large part in the deterioration of our relationship, because the house needed so much work and was constantly draining our energies. Again, communication is essential to maintaining relationships, so if problems occur it's essential to try to talk them through.

A few helpful tips

You will find helpful hints on DIY and decorating throughout this book, but here we have gone into more detail about using tools.

• Most all-purpose hand cut saws have a guide set into the handle. This is marked with the two angles most commonly used when cutting wood, a 90-degree (square) and a 45-degree one.

• When cutting plasterboard to shape, first mark the size that you need onto the sheet. Position a straight edge along this marked line and cut into the plasterboard using a craft knife. You only need to cut through the outer surface. Make sure that you have cut along the whole line, then bend the sheet. It will break, leaving a straight edge. All you need to do then is cut the remaining paper along the break (the other side of the sheet) using the knife.

• If you have lost your nail punch or don't have one, then use an inverted masonry nail. Place the head of the masonry nail on to the top of the nail you want to hide in the timber and hit the pointed end of the masonry nail with the hammer. These nails are made to be driven into concrete and so are very hard and will not bend on you.

• To conceal nails that have been counter-punched into timber, use a bit of putty (brown or white, depending on the colour of the timber) and push it into the hole with your finger. Mould the hole so that it appears to vanish.

• To stop timber splitting when screwing in screws, pilot drill first with a drill bit that is smaller than the screw you are using. This also helps to guide the screw straight. This technique is also useful for little screws such as are used on hinges, which are awkward to hold while trying to screw in straight, and for a neater finish to any job so that the screw's head finishes level to the surface.

Expert advice

 Diary

On the third night we were in the house, the boiler burst and flooded the downstairs living room. This meant we had to remove all the carpets. We had forgotten to break the boiler in gently when we moved in.

There had been only one person living in the house before us, and the radiators were old. When six people suddenly needed so much hot water, all the heaters on the system were overloaded and burst.

We should have been more cautious and only switched a few radiators on rather than all ten. Luckily, the insurance covered the damage.

- To guide your hand saw when cutting, place your thumb against the flat of the saw just above the teeth. Draw the saw back a couple of times to get a slight groove in the timber. It's now possible to start with a normal sawing motion. If you follow the line you should obtain a neat, straight cut.

- Paint brushes with spirit-based paint on them do not have to be cleaned out when you have stopped painting. Just stand them in water up to the stock. This will stop them drying out and keep them malleable for a few weeks. When you need to use them again, just wipe them clean on newspaper. If the bristles are a little hard, dip them in some white spirit.

- To remove excess white spirit or water from your brushes when cleaning hold the brush in the palm of both hands over an old paint pot. Rub your hands together to make the brush spin quickly. This will expel most of the unwanted thinners efficiently, leaving you with a clean brush.

- When hanging wallpaper, expect to see bubbles even if you flattened the wallpaper properly to the wall. They often disappear when the wallpaper is dry, so give the paper a chance to dry out overnight. The more you try to play about with the paper while it is wet, the more likely you are to crease or tear it. If the paper still has bubbles showing 24 hours after hanging, these need to be removed. You can often simply pop them with a pin. If the bubbles are particularly large, then carefully pierce it using a sharp craft knife. This will enable you to peel back the paper to add some more glue, allow the paper to become malleable and re-stick it to the wall using a roller to flatten it. A good instrument for getting the glue through this slice is a hypodermic syringe. Remove any excess glue with a clean, damp sponge.

- And finally, always measure twice and cut once.

 DIY tips

If wallpaper is proving stubborn to remove from a wall try scoring the paper before you soak it with warm water. Using the thin edge of your scraper, carefully scratch through to the wall surface a diagonal line at roughly 100mm (4in) intervals from top to bottom, going from left to right then right to left to give the scored wallpaper a criss-crossed effect. Then apply the water and leave it to soak for 20 minutes. You may need to repeat the water soaking before the paper can be removed. It is important to remain patient and give the water time to soak in. Some people recommend adding vinegar to the water to help loosen the glue.

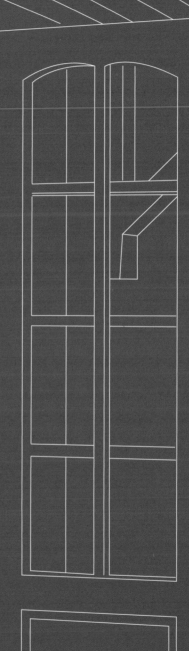

Room by room

>> Living room: introduction

We transformed a dingy and unappealing room into a light-filled and comfortable space for our family to gather in

What we wanted to achieve In our household, the living room is very much a family space. The children have their rooms to do their homework in in peace if they need to; the living room is where we all gather together. It is a focal point of the house, and is where the Christmas tree goes, the television, the piano and a big sofa. Originally this was the darkest room in the house, and not particularly large. I wanted to create a light but comfortable room; one that would allow people to relax in without feeling cramped. The building of the conservatory adjoining the living room greatly increased the light in this area, as well as creating a feeling of more space. I also wanted to create a relaxing and comfortable atmosphere by using tranquil, soft and warm colours such as golds, deep reds and soft greens that harmonise very well. I put in a fireplace to create a focal point (and to create a ledge for special ornaments and family photographs) rather than having the television as a focus, as is often the case in living rooms.

What needed doing We decided to have period-style ceiling mouldings, which meant plastering over the 1970s Artex already in place. Locker and Riley supplied and fitted all the ceiling mouldings in the property. This company has won commissions to fit mouldings in Buckingham Palace and the Houses of Parliament and claim to have the world's largest archive of ceiling mouldings. The design in the living room was manufactured from an original ceiling mould that was a foot in depth. Ours was scaled down to suit the ceiling height of our bungalow. One of the other major tasks was to fit a set of French doors to lead out to the new conservatory. Then the main jobs were to strip off the old wallpaper and hang new paper, sand down the floorboards and varnish them and strip paint off the windows.

Expert advice

Timesavers
Don't bother trying to remove old Artex; you will do more harm than good. Simply plaster over it. You will not need new plasterboard as long as you unibond the old Artex first. Allow twenty minutes or so to allow the unibond to feel tacky on touch. Then use multi-finish plaster to set the ceiling smooth.

Planning tips
When a room needs extensive work, as this one did, it is a good tip to start from the top and work your way down: ceiling, walls, windows, skirting boards and floors.

Living room: what we did

Starting work Once the ceiling mouldings were fitted, we could start on the walls. We stripped off the old wallpaper using copious amounts of hot water. We then chased in new electric cables for the wall lights, using plastic cover strips to protect the cables. The walls were fairly uneven, so we filled in with plaster undercoat and used multifinish plaster to finish smooth. We then fixed the cornices. The cornice comes in three-metre lengths, and it was a craftsman's job to make good the joins. We watched in awe as the Locker and Riley crew used plaster of Paris to carve roses and the moulding pattern to make the join appear invisible. We then unibonded and set the ceiling as described in Timesavers, below left. This is a neck-breaking task as you are bending back and looking up at the same time.

Sealing the walls Our next task was to repair the walls using filler and then rub them smooth. We then sealed all the walls and the new plaster on the ceiling using thinned-down emulsion. Sealing the walls helps with wallpapering as it prevents dry spots, which are caused by moisture from the glue being absorbed into the wall.

Below Once the floorboards were sanded down, we decided to varnish rather than stain them. We used an acrylic varnish that dries within a few hours. Three coats is sufficient to give a good level of protection.

DIY tips
- Sanding floors is a job that produces huge quantities of dust. To prevent dust from spreading around your property, block up as many gaps as you can to contain the dust in one area. Allow the dust to settle before vacuuming up.
- When sanding floors, take a block of wood about the size of your hand and fold a length of sandpaper like a parcel all around it. This allows you to press down hard to get into corners.
- If you need to do any plastering, it is best to do it before sanding the floor. It doesn't matter how many dust sheets you use, plaster residue seems to find its way on to the floor.

Living room: what we did

Stripping paint We had to strip about twenty layers of old paint from the windows because we wanted to take them back to the original wood. There are a number of paint-stripping techniques that you can use. A woodburner will remove the paint quickly, but if you do not learn to use the heat quickly you will scorch the timber and could even start a fire. You can also use electrical sanding DIY tools, although we have never found them particularly useful. Their replacement heads wear out quickly and are expensive to replace. A third alternative is to use a proprietary paint remover. To do the windows, we used a combination of all three methods. We started with the burner for large, flat areas, moving it quickly to avoid any scorching of the timber. Then we used Nitromors paint peeler to get into awkward areas such as corners and grooves. We had several sizes of scrapers at hand, all very rigid. Lastly, we used a sanding

Right I am not keen on PVC windows and chose to keep the old timber-framed windows and restore the leaded lights.

Expert advice

 DIY tips

When stripping off old wallpaper, slash the paper with a craft knife first to let the hot water penetrate. Let the water soak in for 20-30 minutes, and then apply a second coat of water before starting to scrape.

 Details

If you are hanging a wallpaper that picks up the light, make sure that you line the walls beforehand. Otherwise every little bump will be seen.

 DIY tips

If you do not seal new plaster before you paint it (see p.45), the unmixed paint will sit on top of the new plaster and is liable to peel off.

machine to remove any residue and create a soft, smooth finish. Finally, we used Sadolins classic wood stain to seal the wood and bring out the grain.

Opening the doorway We bought a set of French doors and frame from Wickes. This gave us the dimensions for the area to be cut out to allow access from the living room to the new conservatory. First we drew around the frame set up against the wall. We then used an electric disk cutter to cut the brickwork (you must use safety goggles, a dust mask and protective clothing when doing this type of work). After cutting out the shape, we used a hammer and bolster to remove the bricks one by one in order to avoid damage to floorboards and to prevent too much debris flying into the air. The old bricks were disposed of in the skip.

Fitting the glass At this stage the window was ready for the old glass to be removed and be replaced with traditional leaded glass to match the front of the bungalow. Single leaded glass can only be used in old properties as building regulations in new properties do not allow the use of single leaded glass.

Sanding the floor The last messy job to be done was to strip the floor. We hired a heavy duty floor sander and edging sander for the weekend. The merchant will give you plenty of sanding belts, but you will pay only for the ones you return that are not used. Certain techniques are required to obtain a professional finish. Firstly, using the heavy-duty push sander with a coarse-grade-40 paper, move the sander diagonally across the grain of the timber. This should smooth out any rises and bumps on the floor. Never go crossways and do not stop for too long in one area or you will make divots. Next, we used the sander to follow the grain of the timber using various grades of sandpaper, starting with the coarsest paper and then using finer and finer grades. Finally, we sanded the edges using an orbital edging sander.

 Feng Shui

According to Nick, our Feng Shui consultant, the living room was one of the more auspicious rooms in the house. This certainly seems to have been what we have found – this and the conservatory are favourite areas for our family to gather in. We all love it in there. This room is in the northeast sector, which denotes wisdom and education. To improve the room further, Nick suggested that we place a six- or eight-rod wind chime by the entrance to the conservatory.

He also said that the sofa should be placed away from the door and in such a way that we could view people as they entered the room.

Above The lamps in the living room are from Laura Ashley's Ludlow collection. I liked the solidity of them and the finely carved oak-leaf details on the base.

Right Our salvaged fireplace makes an elegant focal point in the living room, as well as offering a stylish base to ornaments and vases of flowers.

Expert advice

Details

I visit local dumps on a regular basis, because one person's rubbish is another's potential treasure. However, it's best to go when you need something specific.

Fitting the doors We installed the door and its frame between the living room and conservatory, and then fitted new skirting. We used a 15cm (6in) ogee type, which we sealed with clear varnish. We then added new architrave to match the skirting. The door from the hallway to the living room was also replaced with a reclaimed and stripped Georgian door. All door and window furniture such as hinges, handles and latches were replaced. For the windows, I chose latches in the 'old monkey' style from Clayton Munroe. These tied in very effectively with the lead in the window glass. Unfortunately, we had run out of light switches from Clayton Munroe at this stage, so we had to do a cunning disguise job. We painted the switch with a gunmetal coating from Polyvine. As long as you use the finest of brushes, you can get away with it. You need to paint when the electricity is off and unscrew the switch so that it is away from the wallpaper.

Painting and wallpapering Our next task was to paint the ceiling and cornice with two full coats of white emulsion, making sure the new floor was covered with dust sheets first. We were then ready to hang the wallpaper. I chose a gold-coloured wallpaper from Sanderson, with details of embossed swirls. This paper has a wonderful sheen that is light-reflecting and helps to brighten the room. It is also a warm but subtle colour that works very effectively as a base hue for the other details in the room. Because the walls were thoroughly prepared previously, it took little time to hang the eight rolls of wallpaper.

Installing the fireplace The salvaged wood and cast-iron fire surround, bought in an antique shop in Saltash, Cornwall, was positioned against a wall to be used at a later date for a wood-burning stove. It was rather rusty when we found it, but we painted it with Hammerite (this is a substance that prevents rusting). We painted the timber mantel in a barley white emulsion, the same colour as the ceiling and mouldings. It proved an eye-catching contrast with the black of the fire surround. We were then ready to bring the furniture in.

Adding atmosphere: the piano and the mirror The old piano was found at the local dump and cost us just a few pounds. It's very twangy and out of tune, but I love the atmosphere that it adds to the room. The mirror hanging above the fireplace is a reproduction one.

The lighting The fixtures in all the rooms were supplied to us by Endon Lighting. The oak leaf lamp on the table from Laura Ashley's Ludlow collection is also available from Endon Lighting.

Living room: the finished room

The sofa I selected a large, coil-sprung two-seater sofa from Furniture Village. This is in a burnished burgundy leather. If you want to buy a new sofa and would like to know how it has been sprung then there is a simple check you can do. Press down on to the front section of the seat and if you can only press down about 15cm (6in), it is a 'fish mouth unit'. If you can push the sofa down a lot further, probably three times further, you have a coil-sprung sofa. Inevitably, the coil-sprung type is far more supportive. Many people, especially those with children, think that it is more cost-effective to buy a cheaper item because the kids will ruin it anyway. However, poor quality sofas last such a short time that they are not really cost effective. A better solution is to purchase a well sprung chair with removable covers so you can replace the covers as they wear out.

Checking old chairs If you are looking to purchase an old chair or sofa and restore it there are a couple of checks you can do to assess whether the item is salvageable or not:

1 If you can push a finger through the top of the seat through the fabric and the backing, the hessian fabric has rotted and will need replacing.
2 Place your hand underneath a chair and feel the base underneath. If it is sagging the springs need replacing.

The window pew There is an old pew that we use as a window seat in the bay window. This originally came from a 400-year-old cottage. The seat, like the timber window frames, had a little white paint residue on them. We left this deliberately as it creates a limed-oak effect.

Soft furnishings and other details The cushions on the linen basket are made from a material from the damask range by Monkwell Fabrics. The crushed velvet is truly luxurious and very expensive. There are large burgundy-red velvet cushions on the window seat, and a variety of cushions on the sofa, in rich fabrics such as velvet and cashmere. For the curtains in the bay window, I chose a soft, sage-green fabric from Laura Ashley. They are full length and sweep the floor. I deliberately left them long to help block out draughts. The fabric that covers the footstool is called 'Sage' from Monkwell's damask collection. The rug is from Laura Ashley and the small chair positioned by the fireplace was one of my salvage bargains – it cost £2 from the dump.

Accessories The glass candlesticks can be found in stores such as Liberty's, Laura Ashley and Mulberry. The plants in their glass pots came from Homebase.

Top Deep reds, golds and greens were the main colours we used in the living room.

Above I like to have lots of homely personal touches, with plenty of vases, plants, flowers and candles.

Left The view of the living room from the hallway door. You can see the double doors that lead into the conservatory.

living roolm

Living room: questions and answers

Q What do you need to bear in mind when deciding what to do in a living room?

A In more general terms, you need to ask yourself what you are going to use the room for. Are you going to be entertaining in there? How many of you are there in the household and how much seating do you need – for example, will you all want to sit down to watch a film together? Is the room dark and do you need to increase the amount of light in there? Will the room be doubling up as a dining area? It can be very awkward trying to place a table in a living room. I keep a table in the corner of the room which can be used for the children to do homework on or for people to eat breakfast off. This table can also be extended out to make room for four extra people.

Q What are good ways to get inspirations for decorating themes?

A My inspiration for the living room was partly taken from visiting antique shops. I love the way you have plenty to look at in antique shops, chests to open, ornaments, pictures heaped chin-high, frames stacked behind chairs. I wanted to recreate that sense of richness and hidden treasures.

Q What are some ideas for possible flooring in living rooms?

A Carpet, laminate and hardwood flooring are probably the most popular options. I personally don't like carpets because I think they present hygiene and cleaning problems. This is a particular issue with us as our family has nine cats! In the living room there was originally a 1980s-style deep-pile carpet. Although it was left in a fair condition by the previous owner, I just didn't know what might be lurking in there. I refused to take my shoes and socks off in there for fear of what might jump out and bite me on the ankles. When we first moved into the

bungalow we laid laminate flooring throughout the house. Although we laid it exactly as per the instructions and used the correct glue, the edges lifted up after only a couple of weeks. In some places the surface started to lift away. Fortunately the supplier gave us a complete refund after a surveyor had viewed the problem. So our personal experience of the material is not good. Laminate flooring is known as a floating floor. It should only be laid on a dead-flat floor. If you intend to lay it over floorboards then I suggest laying down hardboard sheets first. This should give you a fairly flat surface on which to lay it. Laminate flooring is butted together tongue to groove with glue to hold it firm. If a problem should arise underneath the laminate flooring, say with the plumbing, there is no way just a little section can be removed – the whole lot will have to come up. I prefer timber floors because they look attractive, are practical, hard-wearing and easy to clean. They are also not as cold as some people imagine, although obviously they are not as warm and insulating as carpets are.

Q I like the look of wooden floors but also want a room to be comfortable. How can I achieve this?

A One good way is to put plenty of rugs down. I always put a good thick piece of underlay underneath my rugs. Rugs are often thicker than carpets and with additional underlay as well, they make for a very comfortable floor.

Q What is a good way to decide what sort of wallpaper to have?

A The light in the room helped to dictate my choice. The gold wallpaper was brilliant for a dark room. A reflective wallpaper will grab light in the corners, which is what you need in a shadowy room. There is a very subtle print on the wallpaper so as not to make the walls too fussy. I wanted to use the wallpaper as a backdrop for my room, rather than as a focus. That's a point to bear in mind when you are looking at designs – do you want to use them as a backdrop or a feature? You can experiment with more ornamental, dramatic or colourful wallpapers if you have plain furniture. I wanted to have more of a focus on the sofa, which I draped with a blanket throw and cashmere cushions in an assorment of designs and colours.

Q How easy is it to make your own cushions, throws and other accessories?

A It's easier than you might think – this was my experience anyway. I have had no training in dressmaking or sewing, but during my search for sponsors I realised that if we obtained sewing machines we would save money by making our own curtains and soft furnishings rather than buying ready-made items or paying someone else to make them for us. Modern sewing machines are very user-friendly and it is possible to obtain ones with digital display screens. The machine supplied to us was the Brother Galaxy 2100, which is quite an advanced model. At first I dreaded even switching it on, never mind threading it. However, the machine displayed all its functions clearly and told me when the bobbin was running low, when to cut the thread, when to wind the cotton on to the bobbin and how to make buttonholes. Once I had got used to the machine, there was no stopping me. I made the curtains for the master bedroom, the living room and the kitchen. I also made throws for the master bedroom and the piano stool in the living room. My daughter Charlotte made up the napkins in the fabric designed for the kitchen. I also used the machine to embroider a very simple design on the linen tablecloth in the kitchen. Because the design was spaced out along the fabric, it looked very good. It is better to start small and gain confidence and experience with this kind of tool than to try something fiddly and complicated that will take a long time and probably not work that well. This could deter you from trying again. Making your own curtains and throws also gives you the satisfaction of putting your own individual mark

on a room, something that is important to me as a designer – important to anyone who really wants to make a home their own.

Q What are some tips on buying small items of furniture?

A When looking at items such as chairs, I tend to buy things that will work in other rooms. I like the idea of having versatility and being able to make subtle changes to rooms and adapting them. A chair that I rescued from the dump sometimes sits by the fireplace in the living room, but also fits well beside the bath. The linen basket usually sits in front of the piano, but occasionally moves to the end of the boys' bed to be used as a table for their Playstation and games.

Q How do you decide on the best places to position mirrors and pictures?

A I do not like to hang pictures up for a little while, until I have decided on a permanent place for the furniture. You need to allow yourself some settling time before you hang pictures as they can leave light marks.

Q Are there any tips for buying an old piano?

A We bought the piano in the living room just to mess around on and have a bit of fun, so I didn't mind that the piano was a bit battered. If the piano keys stick then it can mean that the woodwork has swelled up and can cost anything from tens to hundreds of pounds to repair. If you know a little about pianos then you will know where to find the soundboard. If the soundboard, into which the tuning pins are embedded, is split, it could cost several thousand pounds to repair. We don't mind the piano being a big clangy and battered – it just makes it more appealing. We might get around to restoring it properly one day.

Harriet's bedroom: introduction

We created a colourful haven draped with delicate Indian silks for our youngest daughter

Above Painting the glitter flowers that give Harriet's bedroom a unique touch. I used embossing glitter. You can buy this in most craft shops – it is generally used to emboss cards.

The challenge we faced Harriet's bedroom was one of the four new rooms that were created when we converted the loft. We put in a large window to create a very light south-facing room – a designer's dream. However, it is an odd-shaped room (see the plan on page 23) with a sloping ceiling. It is also a fairly small room, so it was going to be quite a challenge to utilise the space well. However, we also had the advantage of decorating new walls, with none of the arduous and messy preparatory work that we had to do with the rooms on the ground floor.

What we started with The walls and ceiling were constructed with smooth plaster, and we laid a new wood floor. Paul then made the doors from the remaining floorboards. The wooden floor and door (which we also installed in the other rooms upstairs) created a stylistic unity with the downstairs floor. We also inset a series of halogen spotlights into the ceiling. I really dislike strong lighting, and halogen lights are an ideal solution. They are bright enough to see by – and Harriet uses her room for her schoolwork – but soft enough not to be glaring and too harsh. The halogen lamps give off a little heat too, which is a bonus as loft conversions can be a little chilly in winter. We opted not to fix radiators in the loft rooms and use small loft electric wall heaters. They come in various colours and cost around 2p a day to heat the room.

What we wanted to achieve Starting from what was basically a blank canvas was ideal from a design point of view. When designing a bedroom, one of the most important things to consider is what the person who sleeps in it wants and needs from that room. Think about their personality and how to reflect this in the design. Harriet is very artistic, so we wanted to reflect this and give her a space that would work for her to do her schoolwork, play with her friends and dream her dreams.

The inspiration I also thought back to the room that I had when I was Harriet's age. I wanted a pretty room to play in with my dolls when on my own but that was also grown-up enough to look cool to my friends. Many children tend to have rooms decorated in the style that their parents want, rooms that match the style of the rest in the house. We wanted to create rooms that our children would actually enjoy and want to be in. It seems to have worked, as all of Harriet's friends love this room.

Left The work in progress...creating the glitter stencils was quite a time-consuming and fiddly process, but it was worth it to achieve the overall effect.

The colours we chose The colours that I thought would work best to create the look that we wanted would be those that glow and shimmer in natural light, such as purples and lilacs.

Placing the bed One notable thing about this room was the positioning of the bed. I decided to make the most of the limited space here by placing the bed diagonally in the centre of the room: in odd-shaped rooms the general rule of having a bed beside the wall does not apply. It's an unusual choice, and when Paul and Steve, who helped Paul to construct the bed, were putting the bed in place, they asked me repeatedly if I was quite sure that this was where I wanted it to go. Placing the bed diagonally created a space on the left-hand side, nearer to the window, for Harriet's desk. The space on the right-hand side of the bed was used for Harriet's hanging wardrobe. It is more usual to place a bed against a wall, but that would have created dead space in the room.

Expert advice

 Life tips

One of the inspirations behind Harriet's room came from beautiful Indian fabrics. Our friend who designed the canopy often travels to India to rummage in the fabric markets, and Harriet loves the thought that the fabric was handpicked there. We showed her pictures of Indian bazaars to stimulate her imagination. This is a good way to help a child settle into her room and make her feel involved in the design process.

 Planning tips

It is a good idea to design a room as if it were a clean sheet of paper. Remove everything from the room when you are trying to get initial inspiration, to get a good feel for its shape, space and light.

Harriet's bedroom: what we did

Building the bed Our first major task was to find a bed. Old beds rarely come complete, so I had to settle for buying the headboards only from a local antique shop. Paul and Steve then built the frame.

Painting the floor I decided to paint the floorboards in this room mauve, to tie in with the mauve walls. I love the look of natural wood floorboards, but in this case I thought it would look effective to paint them. However, there are natural wooden skirting boards to break up the lilac of the floors and the lilac of the walls, otherwise it would be rather overpowering.

Painting the flower details One of the most striking features of this room is the glitter flowers that I painted on the wall. First of all the walls were painted with a mauve emulsion. I then handpainted a motif of flowers in a purple glitter over the top, and applied a silver sequin to the centre. I wanted Harriet to catch the shimmer of the sequins in the centre of each flower in the moonlight. It was quite a time-consuming job — it took about a day and a half. I used three colours in my mix for the flowers — red, gold and blue. This enabled me to introduce other colours to the room. For example, the gold blended in with the gold embroidery in the cushions. The overall look is very effective. In fact, people driving past our house at night have asked us whether we have a sunlamp in that room; the room is so light-reflective it looks as if it is ultra-violet!

The furniture I decided to use a mixture of different woods to create a rustic look. Pines, mahogany and oaks can look great together. In any case, most cottagers could not afford to have matching furniture, or had an eclectic mixture of hand-me-downs, so mixing woods creates a more authentic look. There is also a mahogany chest of drawers from Laura Ashley, and an old schooldesk, with a double seat, placed under the window. They are quite rare, so I snapped this one up when I saw it.

Expert advice

 DIY tips

Prepare a box and label it 'paint lid box'. In here keep all your paint tin lids, with their colour name and code. This is useful if you ever need a re-coat some day to freshen up the walls. If you can, order an extra tin, but remember that paint has a shelf life so ask for advice about how long it will keep.

Above A lamp with an ornamental shade and some dried flowers in a vase work well in this pretty room.

Left Harriet's desk and chair underneath the sloping window. There's plenty of light here for Harriet to do her homework.

Feng Shui

Generally, Nick thought that this room was in a good location for Harriet. In particular, he said that studying in this area could help improve academic results – and she has done well at school recently! He thought problems could come from the sloping ceiling, which could cause stress and headaches, and also the fact that the bed was underneath a beam. We countered these bad effects by placing a canopy over the bed. Nick thought the desk was placed badly – it should be arranged so that she can see people coming in. Placing a small mirror to reflect the desk was suggested as a remedy. Nick thought the colours we chose were good, and suggested adding bamboo growing in water to bring further luck to Harriet.

Harriet's bedroom: the finished room

The canopy The canopy over the bed was a major feature of the room. It was made by my friend Harriet, who runs a company called Ribbon Chandeliers. Many of her fabrics are sourced from Indian fabric markets. The canopy is made of a beautiful iridescent purple fabric, partly transparent, and edged with gold. When the canopy is draped over the bed, it is as if Harriet is in a tent.

Bedspreads and cushions To tie the whole room together, we found a wonderful cream bedspread with a few delicate hints of flowers. It seemed as if they had been made especially for Harriet's room. The bedspread comes in cream, but the light reflection makes it appear as lilac. We bought a cushion in Laura Ashley with embroidered petals and sequinned flowers, which tied in perfectly. A tassled cream cushion added extra comfort.

The finishing touches Harriet has a freestanding wardrobe that we bought from Habitat. This has a cream canvas fabric cover and brings a little cream into the room to tone down the lilac. The bedspread was chosen for the same purpose. I did not want to drown Harriet in lilac, but I wanted the flowers to flow around the room. I swagged the wardrobe with a deep burgundy velvet throw to try to coordinate it more with the other colours in the room. The drapery of the throw also echoes the hanging folds of the canopy. I found an old cream porcelain chamber pot, decorated with burgundy-red flowers that I thought would work really well in Harriet's room. I fill it with flowers for her bedside table. Another of my salvage bargains made it into this room; a wooden rocking horse that I bought for a few pounds at a car boot sale. I restored it and painted it a dark purple so it would look at home in this room. For a fun touch, we also hung up a silver glitterball, to add to the sparkle! Then it was over to Harriet, who added her own touches with soft toys, framed photographs of her friends and a slightly battered television.

 Opposite The finished room. You can see how well all the iridescent fabrics and colours harmonise together.

Expert advice

Details

A key feature of this room is the beautiful canopy, made by our friend Harriet. This came with a boning structure to hold it above the bed in a square shape. As the ceiling was sloped I could only use half of the boning structure on the ceiling and tilted the canopy down the back of the wall to cover up the beam. You often have to be versatile with ready-made structures to adapt them to your unique needs and the quirks of your house.

Master bedroom: introduction

Changing the old dining room into an elegant and tranquil main bedroom

 Above Here you can see the soft red paint that we used in the living area that adjoins the bedroom, together with the beautiful fabric we used for the curtains.

The room before This room originally had been the old living room (see plan on p.19). Adjoining it through an archway was an area for dining in that could be accessed only through the lounge. This dining room was an extension that the previous owners had built. I wasn't happy with this set-up. For one thing, I felt that I didn't need a separate room for dining in, and we wanted to use the main space as a bedroom rather than as a living room.

Versatile spaces We like our rooms to be versatile and to offer flexibility in their use. For example, I originally thought that we could use the old dining area as an en suite bathroom. This space could also be used as a dressing room. In future years, the main area could again be used as a living space.

The influence of the decking We built the timber decking at the front of the house in August-September 1999, nearly a year before decorating these rooms. The decking had a strong influence on how we used this area. When the back garden looked like a pony paddock and wasn't at all tempting to sit in, we tended to gather out on the decking at the front. It was pleasant just to sit somewhere that actually looked finished, rather than facing the mess of the rest of the house. It was particularly appealing because the front of the house is south-facing and therefore gets a lot of sun. We came to realise, that, with everyone trooping through this area to get outside, this room made far more sense as a living and sitting area than as a bathroom. This meant that we needed to do some structural work.

Structural changes The old dining area had two windows in it. One looked out on to the neighbour's front garden and the other was high up, set into the adjoining wall. The windows were ugly, not fixed properly and also did not match

Expert advice

Feng Shui

Nick did not think that this was a particularly auspicious room for us to use as a bedroom. In fact, he suggested that we should be in the boys' room, and the boys in here. Nick said that we would be vulnerable to health problems, such as colds and headaches, and both of us have been quite seriously ill in the last year. We had wanted to add a second bathroom here, but Nick warned us not to. Nick thought lilacs would be best in this room, although red was acceptable. Some of the cures he suggested were placing a large plant and a bowl with salt water and coins by the doors to the decking.

the other timber windows that were in the bungalow, so we needed to do something with them. The window that was set high up into the wall we decided to block up. The other window, which looked out to the front of the property, we decided to remove and replace with French doors through which we could gain access to the decking.

Getting rid of the windows Paul removed the original leaded glass from the window carefully, thinking that he might be able to use it later. He also wanted to avoid getting shards of broken glass everywhere when he knocked the window out. The window had been built around on construction of the walls, so it fitted extremely tightly. He had to be careful when removing it because he did not want to damage the facing brickwork to the house. However, it came out with a little gentle persuasion.

Cutting the brickwork The next stage was for Paul to use a disc cutter to cut a straight line in the brickwork to allow for the doorway to be fitted. We hired this tool for the morning for a few pounds. The disc cutter was petrol-driven with a 30cm (12in) stone-cutting blade. It is very important to wear safety equipment when using this tool – any good hire place will offer you the equipment you need for your protection. Lots of dust is produced when using one of these machines, so block up doorways with a dust sheet and make sure you cover anything that you do not want coated in dust.

Fitting the doors After removing the window and cutting further space through the bricks, we had created an opening for the French double doors. The doors came as a complete package with their own door-lining kit. Paul bought the kit before cutting the opening so he could use the measurements from the door lining to cut the correct-size hole. He built the frame on the decking outside from the flat-pack kit and screwed it into the opening, using wall fixings. Before fixing the frame into place, a damp course was placed between the wood frame and the bricks. This prevents water transferring between the two. Bricks naturally absorb water when the rain lands on their surface and this is evaporated off when it stops raining. We then tidied up the interior reveals using a sheet of plasterboard to give a neat, flat finish. Plasterboard is a useful material because it can be easily cut to fill holes using a straight edge and a craft knife.

Removing the chimney breast We had further structural work to do in this room before we could start decorating. There was a chimney breast with a 1950s tiled fireplace that was now redundant. The chimney had been removed at an earlier stage to give us more room in the loft, and the fireplace now served no purpose but instead took up valuable space. I decided to dismantle it one Saturday afternoon while Paul was out playing football. Paul returned home to see dusty smoke pouring out of our open windows. Thinking our house was on fire, he rushed in to find me hammering away at the chimney breast.

 DIY tips
It's particularly important to protect yourself when demolishing old brickwork in case it contains lime. If brickdust gets into your eyes or onto your skin, it can really burn.

 Planning tips
When choosing colours for a room, bear in mind that it is best to use warm hues if you want to create a relaxing environment. Bright colours tend to be stimulating and are best avoided in bedrooms.

 Life tips
We decided to work on the extra living room at a time when we had no family space because we were seeing the negative effects of not having somewhere to relax and talk together.

Master bedroom: what we did

Doing demolition work safely Before starting to knock down the fireplace, I made sure that I was properly equipped, with an all-in-one disposable overall, hard hat, goggles, protective gloves, dust mask, steel-toe-capped boots and a sledgehammer. I had placed Acro props to help support the ceiling near to where I was bashing away. I had also opened all the windows to increase ventilation and put dust sheets around doorways to stop the fine dust from travelling around the rest of the house. Paul helped me to complete the task and to add yet more bricks to the pile gathering on our driveway. It was a sweaty and difficult job, but it was definitely worth doing – it meant that we had an extra room in the loft and a lot more living space in the living room. On the

Below We were originally going to use this space as a bathroom, but then decided it would work better as another living area.

downside, it took us about a fortnight to get rid of all the choking dust and rubble afterwards!

The ceilings Once all the structural work was completed, and the most messy jobs out of the way, we could start the main work of transforming the room. The ceilings, as throughout the property, had been Artexed. Paul sealed them with a coat of unibond, then covered and set them with multifinish plaster to give a lovely flat surface that enhances the Locker and Riley ceiling mouldings. We learnt a lesson here the hard way. The ceiling moulding had already been placed when we came to replaster the ceiling. Really, we should have plastered over the Artex first, as the plasterer's metal tools can chip the mouldings once they are in place. We had to cover the mouldings with masking tape and bubble wrap and be very careful not to do any damage.

Further plastering More plastering was required to straighten up the wall where the chimney breast had been. Paul also had to patch plaster where the window overlooking the neighbour's property had been blocked up. This window was blocked up using bricks that had been removed from elsewhere in the house.

The floors The next step was to sand down the floors, as we had in the rest of the property. We then coated the stripped boards with several layers of a hard-wearing floor-care varnish. We replaced the skirting and architrave with a pattern that would match what we were installing in the rest of the house. We sealed this using clear water-based varnish to enhance the natural grain of the timber. Window latches, door handles and lighting points were replaced with items supplied by one of our sponsors, Clayton Munroe. We were then ready to introduce colour by painting the ceilings and the walls in the sitting area, and hanging the wallpaper in the bedroom area.

Above When deciding which fabrics to use in a room, I like to create a fabric board to see which colours and textures work best.

Expert advice

 DIY tips

If you can, order an extra roll or two of wallpaper. It is important to make sure you have the same batch number, so if you need to make any repairs in the future the wallpaper will match.

 Warning

If you have spare bricks that you are storing outside, keep them covered up. Do not let them become saturated with water, as letting water get into the cement will weaken its bonding strength.

 Details

Cream always goes well with warm colours, while white complements bright, sharp colours.

Master bedroom: the finished room

Above Here you can see what a light-filled room the master bedroom is. It is both elegant and comfortable.

Opposite The living room off the bedroom, which has doors that lead onto the timber decking at the front of the house.

The colours we used As this room is south-facing and therefore very bright, it needed to have warm colours. For the bedroom area, I chose a wallpaper from Zoffany to create a very luxurious look. Zoffany make very high quality wallpapers, paints and fabrics, and most of their collections are inspired by their archive of historical fabrics and wallcoverings. The wallpaper in the bedroom is a warm gold. We applied cream emulsion to the cornice and ceilings. The walls in the old dining area with the double French doors were painted in a contrasting red emulsion. I love the soft red colour. It is soothing to sit here with the double doors open and the sun shining down on the decking outside. The colour also is relaxing and gentle on the eye for reading.

Using the light It's interesting how the light works in these rooms. Both ceilings have been painted barley white, but because the reflected light is affected by the different colours on the walls, one ceiling has a warm gold glow and the other a soft red tinge. This is one reason why it's important to think about how the colours of your rooms work in natural light. Too often, people choose colours by harsh, artificial lighting, and these can look odd or completely wrong when they are applied to the actual room.

Furniture and fittings Once we finished painting, we set about arranging the furniture. We had already planned the positions before we traced and fixed the wall lights. Because of their size, wardrobes can be difficult to place if the wall lights are in the way, so it's always a good idea to think about this before you start working on the room. The bed, wardrobe and bedside tables are from Laura Ashley's Ludlow collection, as are the lamps. The sofas – there is one in the bedroom in the large bay window, and one in the living room – were supplied to us by Figero Furniture. The fabrics on both sofas are from Monkwell Fabrics, as are the curtains on the double doors. The wall lights were from Endon Lighting.

Expert advice

 Details
Elaborate ceiling mouldings add a real touch of elegance to any room. They work particularly well in larger rooms, but can look a little fussy and overwhelming in small rooms.

 Diary
Knocking down the chimney breast was the hottest, dirtiest job I did in this house. It took me half an hour to make even a slight dent in its brickwork with the sledgehammer!

The boys' bedroom: introduction

Creating a cool, uncluttered room with a classical feel

How we wanted to use the room We originally intended to use this room as a guest room, so we wanted to give it a fairly calm, neutral and classical look rather than having it reflect the personality of an individual. However, this has become the boys' bedroom, even though there are enough rooms (thanks to the loft conversion) for them to have a room each. They are so used to sharing a room now that it seems a shame to separate them.

The room before This is a south-facing room, and because of the large bay window it received a lot of light and was particularly hot. It was quite difficult to sleep there on hot summer nights. The room was originally a dark russet colour. I think this colour was chosen to make the bedroom sexy. However, the warm sun on the deep red walls merely made it hard for me to wake up in the morning and definitely did not help my love life (Paul and I slept in here originally before the master bedroom was done). For this reason, we thought that it would only be suitable as a bedroom, whereas the Zoffany room could be used both as a bedroom and a living area. I decided to try to make the room seem more cool-looking through the use of cooler colours and fabrics.

The ceiling moulding The style for this room had to be neither strongly masculine or feminine, so it would be suitable for whatever guests we had. For this reason, we chose a plainer, Regency-style ceiling moulding from Locker and Riley to go in here, in contrast to the more ornate and elaborate mouldings elsewhere in the house.

Stripping the wood Throughout the house we stripped layers and layers of old paint from the window frames to reveal the original wood. This room was the first room we tackled. Paul removed the secondary glazing, and I stripped the

Expert advice

 Feng Shui

This room is in the southeast sector, which represents wealth. According to the Flying Star analysis, the area needed metal. We were advised to use white as a main colour and have metal shelves and ornaments, but to avoid fire colours such

as red. Nick advised us that the best place for the bed was to have it with the foot facing the window, but we placed it opposite the door. To protect occupants from negative energy, Nick advised us to place a screen at the end of the bed.

 Life tips

A lot of people might wonder at our decision to take out the secondary glazing in the window, but we have all had far fewer colds and infections in this house – I think this is because of the increased ventilation.

paint using Nitromors. At first I was very frightened of using this burning liquid, and dressed myself up as if I were about to walk on the moon! The only thing missing was my oxygen tank. I started to get very hot, so removed some of my protective clothing, then accidentally spilt some Nitromors on my hand. I ran to wash it off, half expecting my skin to be peeling off before I got there. It does sting if you get it on your skin, so I learnt not to slap it on so quickly and to leave it for as long as possible to gradually burn through the layers of paint. I also made sure there was plenty of ventilation. After stripping the windows down, I tackled the door in this room.

Above The room before we started decorating it. Paul was most annoyed when I asked him to paint the floorboards white after he had spent so much time stripping them back.

The boys' bedroom: what we did

 Above The deep bay window with its restored leaded glass makes a lovely backdrop for stylish ornaments and plants.

The first stage The first thing we did, as with all the rooms, was to completely clear the room. This meant that we could work on the floor. This bedroom already had a hardwood floor. However, the boards needed some repairs doing before Paul could sand them down.

Preparing the floor After preparing the floor I had a change of plan and asked Paul to paint the floorboards white. He wasn't happy, but I insisted. I understood how he felt. I spent a lot of time stripping the window frames back to the original timber, and then decided that they would look better with a translucent white coating on them to bring out the wood grain.

The floor paint We decided to paint the floor white to help to cool the room down and create the simple, uncluttered look I wanted in here. First of all we tried using the same paint that we had used on the windows – Polar White from Crowns' paint range. However, we found that this took too many coats of paint without looking sufficiently white. It just wasn't effective. The paint was semi-translucent, allowing the wood grain to be seen through. We found these white floors quite difficult to maintain. Anything white – floors, walls, ceiling – can be hard to keep looking pristine, so if you like everything to look perfect then the white floor effect is probably best avoided. I wanted a more solid white look, so we used a basic white emulsion with a protective varnish over the top. I have already painted the floor twice to brighten it up a bit. If I had been comfortable with the aged white floor look I would have used a special white floor paint and then let time do its best – wear and tear makes the look better. Rugs also help to protect the paint and break the floor up a little.

The wallpaper I decided that the room would seem much cooler with a pale coloured wallpaper. I chose a limed oak wallpaper from Laura Ashley. Their fabrics and wallpapers have a lovely natural look. The main colours we used

Expert advice

Planning tips

When we planned what order to do the rooms in, it determined which room would be left to last and therefore which room could be used for storage. It's a good idea to allocate one room for storage. It avoids you having to move things from room to room, where you might damage something that is already finished.

here were subtle beiges and whites, to tone in with the white floor. These colours also created the fresh, cool look we wanted to achieve.

The ceiling moulding We decided to paint the ceiling moulding an antique grey colour, from the Crown Period collection. We then painted the ceiling a warm mauve hue. You should choose subtle colours for ceilings if you decide not to paint them the usual white. The darker the shade you choose, the closer you bring the ceiling to you.

Above This room is elegant and spacious. We've tried to enhance its classical feel by using symmetry; for example, placing matching chairs either side of the wardrobe.

The boys' bedroom: the finished room

The furniture We had lots of antique pine wardrobes and beds, but I decided to have deep mahogany furniture in this room for the visual impact – the relative darkness of the wood looks very striking against the pale floor and walls. The furniture was supplied by Laura Ashley, from their Ludlow collection. There is the bed, matching bedside tables and a chest of drawers.

The bedlinen The bedlinen is plain white and cream, enlivened with purple cushions. The bedcovers are a mixture of embroidered cotton and wool. I find it hard to keep any woven or embroidered bedcovers looking good. They can get pulls easily and the wool tends to bobble. I think it's best to choose prints and cottons for bedlinen. Then you can be more adventurous with throws and cushions. There also are some elegant chairs with purple and cream cushions. To bring all the colours together, I made some floor-length curtains in linen, with bands of colour that tone with all the shades in the room – purple, cream, beige and white.

The bay window One of the most striking features of this room is the large bay window. I like to have curtains fixed to the room side of a bay window, and then have Roman blinds on the inset of the window. Curtains on the outside turn the bay area into a small area perfect for a bench or table to read or work from. I have done this on all the bay windows in the house. It makes the room that little bit more interesting and versatile, and does not make the room seem smaller.

The finishing touches The matting came from Brintons carpets. The curtains, cushions and lights were from Laura Ashley. The fixtures came from Clayton Munroe. The window latches are in the traditional 'Monkey Tail' design.

Above The vibrancy of the purple chair cover looks very effective against all the white in the room and the dark wood of the bedside table and the headboard.

Opposite The overall look. The elegant furniture is from Laura Ashley's Ludlow collection. The floor-length linen curtains framing the large bay window add a touch of grandeur to the room.

Expert advice

Details

- If you are painting a floor white, make sure you know exactly where the furniture is going so you do not get too many scratch marks on the newly painted floor.

- The dark mahogany furniture contrasts very well with all the white in the room. Another wood that would work in here would be dark oak.

Diary

We didn't intend for the boys to be in here permanently, but they seem to have taken to this elegant room. Believe it or not, they even keep it quite tidy.

Bedrooms: questions and answers

Q I have a small house, so how can I get the most out of my bedroom?

A Just because the main purpose of a bedroom is for sleeping in does not mean that that is all you have to use it for. For example, I place a sofa in most of my bedrooms so that I can have an extra space in the house in which to sit and read away from the distraction of the telephone, the children or the cats. In the master bedroom, the small sitting room with doors that lead out to the decking is a great area for reading in. I come in this room when I want five minutes to myself. Everyone needs this special space in their home and it is up to you to create one.

Q What sort of colours are effective to use in a bedroom?

A The bedroom is usually the most personal room in a house (as opposed to being a public room such as a living or a dining room). A bedroom is therefore a good room in which to be a little more adventurous with colours. I often try out new colour ideas in my bedroom first for other rooms in the house as no one gets to see these colours apart from me. As to individual choice of colour, if your bedroom is a very bright room it is advisable to avoid bright colours unless you like to wear sunglasses in bed. Your bedroom should be soothing and restful. You need your rest to tackle the day ahead, so selecting colours that will help you relax is very important. I have found that warm golds create a very soothing effect. Deep, soft reds create a very sensual glow that reflects on your skin. This is why it is thought that deep reds are good for bedrooms and romance. If your room is fairly dark you might want to experiment with more adventurous colours such as soft oranges or warm mauves and purples. If you want to use wallpaper, it is a good idea to choose a subtle, gentle pattern – one that does not shout at you when you come into the room.

Q How can I experiment with different colours before committing to one?

A The most obvious method is to buy small pots of tester paints. However, I think these are quite expensive for what they are, and I don't think you get a particularly good impression of how the colour works overall simply by dabbing a small patch onto the wall. An alternative way to see which colours you like is to buy a selection of coloured light bulbs. They may not give you specific colour shades, but they can give you an idea as to whether you like a colour or not on a much larger scale. Place a lamp with a coloured bulb in the corner of the room. It will light up two walls with the colour that you have chosen.

Q What are other ways to introduce colours into a bedroom apart from paint and wallpaper?

A There are many ways to bring bright colours into your bedroom without keeping you awake at night. You can introduce them using accessories such as lamps, carpets, rugs, bowls or dried flowers in vases. You do not have to splash your favourite bright lemon yellow on the walls. Throwovers are great on beds. It is also effective to have a selection of cushions of similar colours but different fabrics and textures. For example, you might have one cushion in a velvety fabric with tassels, one in a silk or satin, and a third that combines two colours including one that weaves in with another colour you are using in the room. Weaves with a mixture of colours are a great way to introduce other colours to your room. For example, in the master bedroom, the deep red in the bedroom curtains may not be obvious when entering the room, but it allows me to use the same colour in the smaller room with the sofa without looking as if it clashes. I also used this idea in the boys' room, with the long linen curtains that have bands of colour that pick up the shades used in the cushions, chair covers and bedlinen.

Q What are some different ideas for lighting effects in bedrooms?

A I always opt for having a selection of small lights rather than one or two big lights. This makes it far simpler to control the amount of illumination you want in the room. I also like to experiment with different shades. Crisp white lights look very dramatic next to deep colours, and creams work well with warmer, softer hues.

Q How do I do demolition work safely if I need to knock down walls or remove features?

A If you are intending to knock down any walls, enlarge windows to place doors there, or dismantle old features, such as the old fireplace that we removed, there are some important things to take into account. It is surprising how much rubble and dust is created during demolition work, so be prepared for mess and have somewhere to dispose of the debris. Safety is paramount during demolition work and there are several factors to consider:

• If you are knocking down a wall, you need to ascertain whether the wall is supporting roof joists. This can be checked by careful inspection of the loft.

• Disposal of rubble. You will usually need a skip for this. Luckily, our driveway needed to be built up using all the hardcore that we had removed from the house, thus saving us some money.

• Personal safety. You will need to wear gloves, goggles, steel-toe-capped footwear, overalls, dust masks and a hard hat.

• Electric cables or water pipes could pose a problem. There is equipment that you can buy or hire that detects wires and cables that are chased into walls, and you should check before you get the sledgehammer out.

• Always cover floors and any furniture with dust sheets. Plastic ones are the cheapest, but they don't hold onto the dust, so it can be transported to other areas of the property. Also, plastic sheets can be slippery and therefore dangerous, and because they are so light they tend to get moved by a mere opening of a door or gust of wind through an open window. If you don't want to buy new cotton sheets, you can use old bedlinen, although this material won't be as thick as a purpose-made dust sheet. Cotton sheets will stay in place and hold light particles of dust in their fibres, which can then be shaken outside or washed in a washing machine. It is good practice to buy a few good quality cotton twill dust sheets. They come in various sizes and should be large enough to cover the whole floor in the room you are working in. To clean them, shake them off and take them to the nearest launderette.

Q What are some of the most effective methods of stripping wallpaper?

A The soaking method is usually the best. Most wallpapers are made of two layers; the patterned side and the backing part. Using a scraper blade, attempt to separate the two layers. Firmly pull the top layer away from its backing. Next, apply copious amounts of water. Start from the top of the wall and brush down. Allow the water to soak in for 20 to 30 minutes. Then apply another 'coat' of water to just one wall. You can then attack the backing paper with a scraper; it should be fairly easy to remove. An alternative method to remove particularly stubborn wallpaper is to hire a steamer. However, these should be avoided in old houses, because it can make the finish plaster (the top layer) come away from the render. This then causes more mess and other work to attend to, such as replastering. Also, try to avoid using a steam stripper on plasterboarded houses because it can lift the paper layer away from the plaster sandwich material in the middle. In general, a steamer should only be resorted to when the soaking method has failed.

Bathroom: introduction

We created a Victorian-style bathroom with reclaimed wooden panelling, leaded window glass and a slipper-style bath

 Right Paul drew this sketch on the bathroom wall after I had told him what I wanted in there. It's a good idea to have plans like this, even if they are rough!

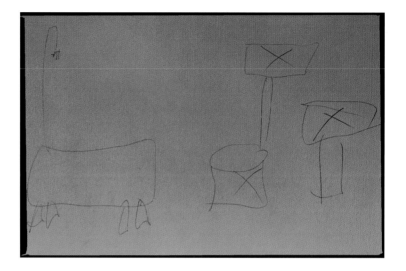

The challenges we faced The bathroom needed extensive work doing to it. However, the room is quite small and the job in here could be contained and completed fairly quickly. In any case, with a family like ours, we needed the bathroom too much for it to be out of action for too long. As it was, we had to cope with using friends' and relatives' bathrooms for three weeks. That was quite a stressful time!

The panelling idea The bathroom measures only 2.5 x 2.1m (8ft4in x 7ft), so it would require a lot of thought to do anything dramatic. I came up with the idea of utilizing reclaimed floorboards as panelling, positioning them up the walls up

Expert advice

 Feng Shui

Nick told us that bathrooms are a problem in feng shui because they always destroy something! However, in our case, the bathroom was in a negative area and therefore destroys some of the potentially bad feng shui problems of the house. We didn't need to add any cures, but were advised to always keep the door shut or any good energy entering the house from the front or the back would continuously be flushed away!

Planning tips

If a bathroom is small (as this one is), it is not a good idea to go for large and chunky bathroom furniture. The bathroom suite we chose gives a feeling of space and the illusion of a larger bathroom.

to a height of around 1.5m (5ft). Paul wasn't keen on this idea because, when he looked at the materials, he realised they had seen better days and would require a lot of work to make them look effective. The floorboards we bought were 18cm (7in) wide. Because of the width, Paul thought that they would bring the room in even more. Actually, when it was completed, the panelling had the opposite effect, particularly as we painted the top half of the wall Barley White, which pushed the walls out and made the room lighter.

The problems of the layout One of the main problems with this room was its size, so the layout – where all the fixtures such as the bath suite, hand basin and toilet were placed – could not be changed. It would be physically impossible to fit the bath other than against the longest wall. As a professional decorator, Paul has worked on many jobs where a client has bought a bath only to find that it doesn't fit in the space. We also wanted to hang the door the other way because originally the first thing you saw was the toilet. This didn't matter when the old suite was in place, but the Albion Bath company was supplying us with a Victorian-slipper bath, which would be a far more attractive feature to see first.

Left The bathroom as it was before, with outdated tiling, a 1980s bathroom suite and an ugly window.

Bathroom: what we did

Below This is one of my favourite finds. This antique cast-iron fire surround covers up the radiator and also provides a handy ledge.

The first tasks We stripped out the existing 1980s bathroom suite to clear the space for our Victorian reproduction suite. We had originally considered refurbishing an original Victorian or Edwardian cast-iron bath, but we discovered that this would have been too heavy for the existing floor structure.

Working on the entrance With the room clear, we could rehang the door. Even simple things like this can make a tremendous difference to a room when you enter it. To rehang the door, Paul had to move and reposition the locks, hinges and handles. This is quite a simple job and only basic carpentry tools are required, such as a screwdriver and chisel.

Rehanging the door Firstly, you need to remove the handles. This will allow you to remove the latch and change it around so it can be pushed closed. Then replace the handles. Next, unscrew the door from the door frame. It is easier to unscrew the hinges on the door frame first because you can push as hard as possible and the frame won't move, whereas the door will move if you try to unscrew the hinges to the door when it is still swinging on the door frame. This makes it hard to exert the pressure that is sometimes needed to undo screws in a door. If the screws that hold the hinge to the door or door frame are painted or rusted firmly in place and don't seem to move no matter how much effort you use, place an old screwdriver in the slotted part of the screw and hit the screwdriver firmly with a hammer a couple of times. This will break the paint seal or rust bonding, allowing you to remove the screws.

The next stage Reposition the hinges to allow the door to be opened on the new side of the frame. Mark around the hinge with a pencil and chisel out the timber so that the hinge lays flush with the door edge. Do the same on the door frame. Once the hinges have been attached to the door, it is possible to hang the door in the frame.

Expert advice

 Diary

One of my most vivid memories of the project was the day when we finally had lights in the bathroom. It was such a novelty that we all stood and took turns switching the light on and off!

 DIY tips

If you are thinking of using solid fixtures, as we did, to hang your curtains, be warned that they are rather heavy. The company that you are buying the products from should be able to give you advice on what fittings will work best on whatever type of wall you have, such as plasterboard, cob, brick, timber or cement, and will be able to advise you on weight capacity.

Stopping the water We shut off the water to enable us to rip out the old bathroom, leaving an empty shell. We put valves on the end of the pipes so that we could still have running water into the kitchen. When we eventually came to fit the bath it would be a simple matter of connecting to these valves, allowing us to have a switch-off point to each item in the bathroom.

Replacing the window The window had to be removed because it wasn't in keeping with the rest of the property. It was of a metal frame design with horrible shell carved glass. We bought a wooden frame window with leaded glass from a reclamation yard. This was 300 years old and had come from a demolished cottage. It was slightly smaller than the one we removed, but with a bit of making good to the walls we managed to fit it in position. I thought that the smaller window would give more of a cottage feel from the inside. Paul made good the walls around the newly installed window using plasterboard to fill any gaps.

 Above, Louise touching up the antique fire surround that disguises the radiator. Restoring your own finds is truly satisfying.

The panelling To construct the panelling, Paul battened the walls horizontally every 20cm to a height of 120cm (8in x 48in) from the ground using roofing battens. He then cut the floorboards to the correct height and nailed them vertically to the battens. Next, Paul sanded the boarded-out area using an orbital sander, working through various grades to get a smooth finish. After this the timber was varnished and sealed with a treatment from Polyvine.

The flooring We had to rip out the flooring in the bathroom and replace it with reclaimed floorboards because the originals were completely rotten. It might sound as if the wood is overpowering in this room, but it works and is practical. It's all thoroughly sealed and varnished because of all the water likely to be splashed about in there. I prefer wood to tiles because it lasts longer. With tiling you need to replace the grouting every few years.

 Timesavers

If you need to turn the water supply off while working on a bathroom, make sure you know where your stopcock is. Paul had to dig around for an hour in the grass verge outside before he found ours!

 Life tips

Having a bathroom out of action is one of the things that most disrupts family life. This is one case where you really have to be prepared to rough it. We had to troop off to friends' houses whenever we needed a wash, and we also took to going to the local swimming pool for a shower. We all felt like tramps for a while!

Bathroom: the finished room

The paintwork and panelling The ceiling and the walls above the boarding were painted with white emulsion and then varnished over using an acrylic Polyvine varnish. This helps to prevent moisture from damaging the paintwork. When the wall panelling was sanded down and varnished, it took on a pinkish sheen, which looks warm and weathered, and is very well offset by the gleaming white paint above it.

The bathroom suite We installed an Albion slipper bath, hand basin and toilet. The toilet is notable for its high-end cistern. I particularly liked this because it helped to open up the space in this small room; it leads your eye from floor to ceiling. The toilet had a pretty, decorative hallmark inside. Unfortunately it says 'Charlotte', which is the name of our eldest daughter. This prompted lots of teasing from our other children.

The fixtures and fittings Accessories for door and curtains were supplied by Clayton Munroe. The curtains I found in a sale box at Laura Ashley. I was guessing when I bought them, but I was pretty certain that they would fit our reclaimed windows perfectly, and I was right. I'm lucky in having a very good eye for judging distance and measurements, which certainly comes in handy when I'm out at salvage yards and car boot sales looking for bargains. I'm usually very good at judging what items will fit where. However, if you don't want to take a risk, carry a note of measurements around with you.

Mirrors and pictures The large mirror above the fireplace is made from antique pine. It is mainly used to reflect the picture from the other wall. We hung it horizontally to maximise the space and to try to make the room appear larger than it is – every little helps! There are not many pictures in our house; I often prefer to hang mirrors up because I like to play with light and reflections and the interesting effects that these create in rooms. The picture behind the cistern pipe we got from a car boot sale for a few pounds. It's a copy of a famous Pieter de Hooch painting.

The radiator cover Perhaps my favourite item in this room is the radiator cover. When Paul was battening the walls he worked out his measurements so that the reclaimed timber, when fixed, would be flush with the old radiator. Once this was established all I had to do was to search a reclamation yard for a small antique cast-iron fire surround. The one I found fits perfectly and can easily be removed should there be any plumbing problems. The fireplace also had the added bonus of giving us an extra shelf.

Below This room is quite small, and to try to make it seem bigger we put in the high-end cistern, painted the upper halves of the walls white and placed the mirror horizontally.

Opposite The finished room. The high back to the Victorian-style bath stops the water spilling over the edge when you push yourself upright from a relaxing soak.

Bathroom: questions and answers

Q **What is a good way to tackle the complete decoration of a room?**

A Paul recommends the following step-by-step process:

- Always work on a room from to top to bottom. First ascertain what needs to be done to the ceiling. For instance, most ceilings tend to have cracks with flaking paint on them, so scrape it off using a 5cm (2in) or 7.5cm (3in) flat scraper. Then, using the edge of the scraper, open up the cracks to a V shape. This allows more filler to be placed in the crack, stopping the crack from reappearing. Allow the filler to fully dry before rubbing down smooth.

- The next job is to tackle the walls. If they have been wallpapered, this needs to be stripped off to expose the bare walls. Prepare the walls by filling holes and rubbing them down smooth. If you are going to hang fresh wallpaper, size the walls first with thinned-down paste and allow it to dry. If you are just going to paint, then seal the walls with some thinned-down emulsion.

- While you're working on the walls, the ceiling filler has had time to dry. Rub it down and seal over the filler marks with neat emulsion. Apply two full coats over the whole area, cutting in the edges using a 5cm (2in) or 7.5cm (3in) brush, then rolling the large areas in the middle. A roller on a broom handle really speeds up this process. With the windows open giving plenty of ventilation, it is possible to give the ceiling a second coat on the same day.

- When the walls are sealed, this helps to highlight any defects that may require filling. Spot these over with neat emulsion to seal the filler. Now apply two full coats of emulsion to the walls. Cut in the edges with a brush, leaving the large areas for the roller. To prevent the roller from drying out if you need to leave the job for a break or overnight, place it in a plastic carrier bag

and wrap it tightly. This will prevent air from getting to the paint and drying it out.

- With the ceiling finished, it is easier to cut the wall in to where the wall joins the ceiling. If the woodwork in the room is to be painted, I paint emulsion on to it to a level of about 10mm. This does not have to be accurate because I am confident in my abilities as a decorator to know that I can tidy this up when I come to paint the woodwork.

- Prepare old painted woodwork by rubbing it down with sandpaper. Remember to wear a dust mask because old paint often contained lead, which you do not want to breathe in. You do not have to rub down so that the bare wood shows through underneath, but only to give the undercoat a key. This means scratching the old paintwork enough to enable the next coat to adhere, so preventing it from peeling.

- With the woodwork preparation complete, the next stage is to undercoat any windows, doors, skirting boards and architrave. This should be allowed 24 hours to dry before the top coat is applied. The last stage is to gloss the undercoat.

Q **Are there any tips on tiling?**

A Tiling is a popular choice for bathroom floors and ceilings because it is water-resistant, hard-wearing, easy to maintain and easy to clean. It can be somewhat cold, however, particularly under foot, and this is one of the reasons why we chose to have a well-sealed wooden floor in our bathroom instead. One thing to bear in mind when laying tiles is that it is rare for walls to be perfectly flat, particularly in older properties. It is therefore particularly important that you lay the tiles onto a ridged layer of adhesive. The ridges allow the tiles to be adjusted so that they lie flat both relative to the wall and to the previous tile. Adhesive that is applied flat to the wall does not allow for this adjustment. Waterproof adhesives should be used around showers and baths. Pre-mixed adhesives are available on the market. They are relatively more expensive than the brands that you mix yourself, but you can be sure they are the right consistency and will save you time on the job overall. When you are estimating how many boxes of tiles you need to complete a job, always add on an extra five per cent in case of breakages and to set aside for repairs in the future.

Q What are the advantages of having an electric shower installed?

A Electric showers have two main advantages: they are economical (a shower can save you a third of the water that you would use for a bath) and they provide hot water whenever you need it. You also save energy by not heating stored water, because the shower heats the water instantaneously. When you are looking at different models, check out the wattage. The higher the shower's wattage, the better the performance of the shower. Electric showers are relatively easy to install. They only need a connection to mains electricity and a single cold-water pipe running from the rising main. However, unless you are very confident in your skills with wiring, it is best to have a professional electrician to connect the wiring at the consumer unit. Be aware that there are certain water bylaws on plumbing installations. Contact your local water board to make sure what they are and whether they affect you. For example, there are requirements on anti-syphon valves being fitted to shower installations where the shower head may reach below the top of a bath.

Q What is an easy and inexpensive way of giving an old bathroom suite a new lease of life?

A Changing the taps on your sink and bath is a simple way of updating the style of your bathroom. It is a relatively easy job to do yourself. Possibly the most difficult aspect of it is removing the old fittings. In older suites they

may have been puttied into place, so they may need a bit of brute force to remove them. Space is often limited in bathrooms, so you may also face the extra challenge of not having much room for manoeuvre. While you are changing your taps, you might also want to change other small fittings such as toilet roll holders, toothbrush holders and towels rails. It can be surprising what a change can be achieved from just updating these accessories.

Q How practical is it to have a wooden floor in a bathroom?

A It is perfectly feasible to have a wooden floor in a bathroom. You just have to take particular care to seal and varnish it to give it adequate waterproofing. It is also possible to get a good quality laminate flooring that has been specially designed to go in a bathroom. Other ideas are quarry tiles, which look very attractive and are very durable, but can be expensive. A cheaper alternative is vinyl flooring, which is highly water resistant and very economical. Vinyl flooring is very easy to lay if you are not particularly experienced or confident of your DIY skills. You can get vinyl tiles or you can buy it in rolls so you can cover the whole room in one go.

Q What factors should I take into consideration when choosing a new bath?

A One of the most important things to take into account is the amount of space you have in your bathroom, especially because bathrooms tend to be one of the smaller rooms in a house and can often feel cramped. A lot of people overlook this and end up buying a bath that is too big. You have to make sure that there is room for you to get in and out, room for you to open and close the door, and space for you to dry yourself when you get out of the bath. Then you have to select what style of bath you want, such as a corner unit or a freestanding one. You also need to choose taps to go with the bath, and check that they fit the tap holes on the bath.

Kitchen: introduction

Storage space, safety and hygiene are the main factors to take into account when planning kitchen refurbishment

Initial plans Our kitchen needed a major overhaul. Originally, the kitchen was a 3m x 3m (9ft x 9ft) ro ked out that the kitchen was last refurbished in the early 1980s – it was decorated with beige wall tiles, beige Formica worktops, beige kitchen units and beige floor tiles that wobbled when you walked on them. Everything in the kitchen needed replacing – doors were falling off the units, and water had got under the surface of the Formica worktops and bubbled the surface away. There was no way I wanted to cook or entertain in a room that felt so unhygienic.

Planning the room Each room in my home, and in any home that I design, has a purpose, and I like to keep it that way – for example, no eating in bedrooms! I thought about what I wanted to use the kitchen for. I like to entertain, but only on special occasions. I felt I could easily put a table in the conservatory for that situation – I did not need a room just for eating in. My children have different timetables and come and go according to their sports, schools and friends. Therefore my kitchen generally needs to serve only as a snack or breakfast bar.

Considering storage space We are a fair-sized family, so storage space is very important. I don't have time to shop three times a week, so I needed plenty of cupboards in which to house provisions. I also decided to put in a breakfast bar. This helps to control the traffic in the kitchen – it forms a sort of barrier so people can't wander into my food preparation space. I salvaged an old shop counter to use as the breakfast bar. It also has plenty of storage space under it.

Safety issues Safety is the most important issue to consider when designing a kitchen. I wanted to avoid having islands with hotplates in the centre of the

Expert advice

 Life tips

We wanted our kitchen to be the focal point in the house, but this did not work because it was too small a room. We would make our lunch and then disappear into the lounge to sit in front of the TV.

This meant that communication within our family quickly deteriorated. If you are losing a family room for a while, make sure you find a temporary replacement. Communication is vital when

you live on the job. It's tough work that makes you tired and grumpy when things go wrong. If there is nowhere to flop out together then you end up with problems – lonely children and lonely adults.

kitchen unless there was a lot of workspace around the hotplate or burners. The placement of the cooker was also important. I did not want to carry hot pans to drain water from potatoes to a sink on the other side of the room. When deciding where to put the cooker, I needed to think about traffic routes into and around the kitchen; where the door is, where people can walk to, what they walk past and how much space there is.

Lighting Choosing lighting was also a safety issue. I need to be able to see what I am cooking, and more importantly, whether it is cooked. However, I did not want to dazzle myself or my neighbours in the process. I decided to have halogen lighting installed. These are strong without being harsh.

Flooring and worktops There are important hygiene issues with flooring. Carpets cannot be bleached and are never truly clean no matter how much you vacuum. That's why I chose to have wooden floors in nearly all the rooms, including the kitchen. I am also not keen on work surfaces with grooves, such as tiled worktops. They look good, but are difficult to keep hygienically clean. I decided to have wooden worktops, as they are attractive, hygienic and practical. We coated them with varnish to protect them against moisture.

Above The kitchen mid-refurbishment. It wasn't a particularly appealing area to prepare food in, so we relied quite heavily on takeaways for a while!

Kitchen: what we did

 Above Our builder, Steve, fitting the wooden worktops for the new kitchen.

Getting the experts' advice Because we had so many issues to take into consideration, and so many things to change in the kitchen, we talked through our ideas with our plumber and electrician. They advised us on safety and practical issues, such as where to put plug sockets. Cookers, sinks and washing machines were found homes first. Then we had to think about where to place the sink and the worktops to optimise the space.

Siting the sink The original sink was only partially under the window and had only one sink and a drainer. We wanted to change the layout so we could put a double sink right under the window. This allowed for more working space between the cooker and the sink. I really wanted to have two sinks in this kitchen, one for cleaning food and the other for dirty dishes. I did not have enough room for two sinks and a drainer, so I bought a wooden slatted drainer that we modified to fit on top of one of the sinks. When we cleaned up after preparing food, the drainer went on the food preparation sink and the plates went on the drainer. This freed up more worktop space and also meant I could see into the garden when preparing food. However, this can be a distraction now as I tend to focus on all the weeding that needs to be done!

Enlarging the room Once we had done our extensive planning, we could set about the building work. The kitchen was quite a demanding job because we had demolition work to do here first to enlarge the room. The kitchen was next to a small room that had been used as a bedroom (see plan on p.19). By the time we started the kitchen we had already done some remodelling in this area. Some of this room had been used for the stair access to the loft rooms, and for the creation of a utility room with a door leading outdoors. The rest of this space allowed for the kitchen to be enlarged by 2m (6ft6in). All that had to be done was to remove a solid single brick wall about 3m x 2.5m (9ft x 8ft). With the demolition work completed, the kitchen had almost doubled in size.

Expert advice

 Life tips

One of the biggest problems encountered in DIY, especially with a large project like a kitchen, is the fact that it's never going to be done in a weekend. You have to be prepared to rough it for a bit. In our case, the launderette and takeaway did some good business from us for a while. It's funny how the seemingly simple task of cooking in one's own kitchen becomes a distant dream, and another unexpected money drainer.

 Planning tips

When reorganising a room, a good tip is to draw a plan of the room on a piece of paper. Make paper models of your furniture to move around on the plan to get an idea of how best to fit them in and use the available space.

Changing doors and windows We remodelled the space by blocking up the back door. Our access to the outside was then created by a doorway from the utility room. We removed the old patio doors that had led into the garden and replaced them with a single cottage-style door and a window next to it. We also created more light and space in the kitchen and the hallway by fitting double doors between the hallway and kitchen. These created more space in the hallway because the old doors had opened out into the hallway. We changed the way the doors hung to be more efficient. These doors were salvaged from an old nunnery, and the top half is made of glass. I kept the old saftey glass in them because I liked the criss-cross effect.

Below The kitchen before we blocked up the old doorway. You can also see the dresser as it was before we painted it.

Kitchen: what we did

Changing the floor levels We then had to address the problem of the floor levels being different between the kitchen and the small room. The kitchen had been cast in concrete, while the small room had conventional floorboards. The kitchen was 15mm (½in) lower. Paul had some roughcut timber cut to that size and screwed it to the concrete floor. We thoroughly preserved the timber first, as it was in an area that was likely to have large amounts of water splashed on it. We then placed tongue and grooved floorboards across the battens and nailed them into place.

The next stages Before we levelled the floors, we removed the old kitchen units. Next, our plumber and electrician sorted out our new plumbing requirements and re-wired the kitchen. Then we could fit our new kitchen units and appliances. By this time the kitchen was starting to take shape. With the

Right Paul painting the MDF tongue and grooved sheeting, which was fixed to battens on the kitchen walls.

Expert advice

Moneysavers
Be careful about what fabrics you use in the kitchen. They need to be quite sturdy. Certain inexpensive imported fabrics, in my experience, are only suitable for items that will not be washed much. Some of

the fabrics I have bought in the past were not colourfast and faded in sunlight. Also, prints are better than weaves for most upholstery, as weaves can catch easily.

Details
I bought the breakfast bar – originally a shop counter – in an antiques shop. I loved the tongue and grooved effect on it, which tied in well with the walls.

main items in place, we were ready to fix tongue and grooved MDF to the walls and install the wooden worktops, made from lovely ash timber.

The salvaged beam When we removed the wall between the old living room with double doors onto the back garden and the kitchen, I wanted to keep a visual divide between the two rooms. People quite often achieve this effect by making an archway. I didn't want to do this, but I did want a break-off point from the kitchen to the walk-through area for the utility room. I decided to have a recycled ceiling beam there instead. The beam was salvaged from a cottage that was about four hundred years old. It works really well over the antique shop counter, which we now use as a bench, storage centre, work surface and serving bar. The rustic look of the kitchen is enhanced by the beam; it helps me to create the atmospher that I am in a cottage kitchen rather than a fifty-year-old bungalow.

The reclaimed doors We used reclaimed wooden doors in the kitchen. These tend to have gaping holes where the locks and handles have been removed, and this takes skill and time to put right. However, the benefit of reclaimed timber is that it has matured and dried, bent and twisted about as much as it will before you fix it in place. At first, we had installed new doors, but within only a couple of months they had warped and would not close properly, thus wasting us money.

The reclaimed window The window was another reclaimed item, and was a real labour of love. It cost one tenth of the price of a new one. It took a little longer to fix – it had to be jigged about by an experienced builder in order to fit the damp course already in the walls of the house – but I think we saved money on it overall. We used old stair treads for the window ledges for both windows in the kitchen.

 Above, Near to the end of the project, when every minute counted, I had to call in every helping hand I could. Here, Martin is repairing the dresser before I painted it.

 Warning
When stripping paint, leave the stripper on for as long as possible. It's always tempting to start scraping off the paint to get a glimpse of the wood, but be patient. Nylon brushes will melt, but then the chances are that whatever you use will be unusable again, so don't bother buying expensive brushes. You also need a good scraper that gets into the corners and scrapes the flat surfaces.

Details
The salvaged wooden beam in the kitchen is not structural – it was installed for visual impact only. However, it makes a great hanging base for pots and pans.

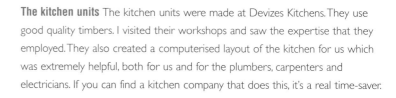

Kitchen: the finished room

The kitchen units The kitchen units were made at Devizes Kitchens. They use good quality timbers. I visited their workshops and saw the expertise that they employed. They also created a computerised layout of the kitchen for us which was extremely helpful, both for us and for the plumbers, carpenters and electricians. If you can find a kitchen company that does this, it's a real time-saver.

The dresser I decided to paint the wooden dresser, which upset nearly everyone. However, what with the timber kitchen units, timber floors and timber windows, there seemed to be an overwhelming amount of wood in the room, so out came the paint pot. I painted it a soft yellow, which was also the colour of the walls. It adds a very light and airy feeling to the kitchen, and helps to create the welcoming atmosphere.

The curtains For the kitchen curtains I chose a French fabric from Tissunique. It has a stonewashed appearance that will look better with age. Linen also looks better as it is washed and used, and you will no doubt wash kitchen curtains more than others. When you buy curtains, make sure you ask the retailer how colourfast your fabric choice is. A good fabric retailer will also be able to advise you which fabrics are good in sunlight. There's nothing worse than sun-faded lines on your curtains. To colour coordinate the room, I had the fabric scanned and then took it to a DIY merchants to have a paint made up to match.

The pottery The pottery was made at Purbeck Pottery in Poole. We cut templates from the pattern on the fabric, and left them to make a glaze to match the fabric. They said that it takes a long time to get a glaze right, but we had a good match within three tries, and were most impressed with the results.

Fixtures and fittings All the fixtures and fittings, such as door handles, window latches and curtain rods, came from Clayton Munroe.

The overall effect The kitchen works brilliantly for us, and I know it would work for anyone else if we ever have to sell. Even the children love it, and that's saying something. It is warm and inviting, practical and hygienic, with work surfaces that are easy to clean. There is plenty of storage space and preparation space. And the utility room is an added bonus – an area we use to contain mess. The cats' food bowls and litter tray are in here, together with coats, shoes and outdoor clothes that would otherwise clutter the hallway.

Below Details are important when designing a room. Having the curtain fabric and the pottery made up in the same colours and patterns gave the kitchen a really harmonious feel.

Right We bought the dresser in an antiques shop. It had been dipped to remove all the old paint, which is not always the best option. Dipping destroys the old glue and can end up leaving furniture looking as if one knock would make it fall apart.

Kitchen: questions and answers

Q Can you save money by purchasing a second-hand kitchen?

A You only really save money if you can fit it yourself. Many people look for kitchens the same size as their own. There are always problems with removing kitchens. Edges can be damaged, screws may not unscrew and damage the cupboard base. My advice is to look for a kitchen with more units than you need. It will give you more flexibility. The sink will probably not be in the same position as yours and therefore the worktops will not be right for the final shape of your kitchen.

Q How can I revamp my old kitchen tiles?

A The most affordable and effective product I have found is 'Tile Magic'. You will need to make sure that there are no breezes to blow anything on the paint as the effect is easily ruined by dust or specks. Apply the paint with a roller rather than a brush to get a smoother effect. Do not roll on too much paint as any drips will make the job hard to rescue. If you have kitchen tiles that have a raised pattern surface you may need a few base coats to make the surface smooth before applying your chosen colour and then varnishing. Make sure that you leave paints to dry for the recommended drying time between coats. Tile Magic is also effective for enamel baths.

Q Can I save money by fitting my own gas appliances?

A It is illegal to fit any kind of gas appliance without a Corgi Registered Certificate. Always pay a professional to do such jobs.

Q What are the advantages of having a computerised kitchen plan done before I buy?

A Many kitchen showrooms now offer a computerised printout of how your kitchen will look, and these are very useful. The showroom will need accurate kitchen measurements in order to produce a plan. It is a good exercise to do to find out what space you have for cookers, washing machines and any other appliance, and how best to use the space. Our kitchen plan was very helpful. It showed the electrician where to fix cooker sockets and where best to fix plug sockets. It also enabled us to mark out where the recessed light fittings needed to go.

◀ **Left** The kitchen completed. The old shop counter, which we use as a breakfast bar, and the tongue and grooved walls, tie in well with the timber floorboards.

◀ **Above** The door handles offered us a few unconsidered surprises. The handles were so heavy that it took a couple of attempts to get the right latches so the handles would not keep hanging down.

Conservatory: introduction

Extending our home involved turning a damp haven for spiders into a light-filled and comfortable space where we could sit and see the sky

 Above We thought that the conservatory would be the ideal place for the aromatherapy steam capsule. This is perfect for when we've got colds – we just sit in there and sweat them out.

Our starting point We wanted to remove and replace the existing extension, which had been built by the previous owners. It had been built rather poorly, with only a single-skin brick wall with no cavity and insufficient footings (foundations for the walls) and a roof made of corrugated iron, which leaked badly. It also had a sloping floor that drained into a gully, which was always full of water. The area was basically uninhabitable as nothing in it could be kept dry. We had to get rid of it as it was hazardous, not to mention a severe eyesore. We could have extended the house into this area, but we would have needed planning permission to do so. Another factor to take into account was that we were looking for ways to increase the natural light in the house. The living room, which is at the rear of the house and faces north, was one of the darkest areas. Building a conservatory on to it seemed like a good way to increase the available light, as well as enlarging the living space for our family.

Our first ideas The area next to the rear half of the garage was originally a bedroom, which we had converted into the new living room. Our original idea was to extend into the rear of the garage and replace the walls. However, we decided to replace the walls and extend them out into the garden. Instead of having a standard flat roof, we thought a conservatory roof would be better, and by fitting a double door from the living room to the conservatory area we would let in much more natural light. We also decided to build a wall alongside the fence line of the garden. We did this for three reasons: so that the fence would not be visible from the conservatory; to make the conservatory feel more part of the house by using a full-height wall; and thirdly for privacy reasons. We also wanted a glass roof so we that we could sit in the

Expert advice

Planning tips

We were advised that there would be no planning problems so long as our conservatory did not exceed 10 per cent of the overall house area dimensions and was accessed only via the double doors

from the house. There must be a double doorway separating the house from the conservatory to exempt your conservatory from being classified as an extension. If you do not do this, you are

likely to require planning permission. Building regulations apply to all buildings work, replacement or new.

conservatory at night and see the stars. There are various types of glass roofing available; we opted for a tinted roof glass, which takes away the glare of the sun while still allowing us to see out.

Finding the right supplier We approached several companies for ideas and inspiration for our conservatory. One company stood out from the rest; Portland Conservatories, who are based in Manchester. They are professional and experienced. They offer advice on how best to utilise your area, where to place doors, roofing options and most importantly whether you will need planning permission.

Negotiating the price Our next step was to negotiate the cost of the conservatory. Although Portland offer a complete package from design to completion, we decided to save costs by having Paul and Steve, our bricklayer, build the base. This left Portland to fit and build the conservatory framework. We also decided that Paul and Steve would complete any remedial work such as laying the floor, plastering, painting and fitting light switches.

Above left View looking along the rear of the house at the completed conservatory. You can see how the conservatory protrudes out from the bungalow, and how it leads out onto the timber decking.

Above right We also have an infra-red sauna in the conservatory.

Conservatory: what we did

Preparing the site We knew that we would have a lot of rubble and waste material to dispose of because of the demolition work, so we ordered a skip. These come in various sizes depending on the amount of waste to be disposed of. Once the demolition was underway, we placed old bricks to one side to use as hardcore for the base of the conservatory. Corrugated sheeting, rotten timber, windows and doors and anything that could not be reused were placed in the skip.

Levelling the floor Our next task was to level out the sloping floor at the rear of the garage. We worked out from the plans that these levels would have to be reduced down to the correct height for the building of our conservatory base. We hired a concrete breaker, at £15 a day, to crack the concrete. Once the site was levelled we could start the building work.

 Right Here you can see the use of string liner set upon profiles. We used this process to transfer plan dimensions accurately from paper on to the area where the proposed conservatory was to be built.

Expert advice

☠ Warning

To carry out demolition work in a safe manner you will need adequate safety equipment. Essential items should include:

- a hard hat
- rigger gloves. These have a leather palm with a cotton backing

- steel-toe-capped boots. These will protect your feet in case you drop something heavy on them. Trainers will not protect you at all
- a dust mask to filter out harmful dust particles

- safety goggles to protect your eyes from splinters or fragments – for example, if you are smashing something with a sledgehammer

The building work Referring to the plans, we set up four profiles. These are made by placing three vertical stakes into the ground about a metre apart in a 90-degree square joined by two horizontal pieces. From the air this would look like the letter L. These were placed at the corners of the conservatory, about one metre beyond the maximum dimension. Once placed in the ground we did not want to disturb them until the building was underway.

Using the profiles The profiles are used to run string lines from. These enabled us to transfer the dimensions from the plans on to the site (ground) accurately. It was essential to get this stage correct to the nearest millimetre because we were having a bespoke conservatory frame built in a factory and then assembled on site. The horizontal bar on the profile allowed us to move the string line to the exact measurement on the plans. We set up the profiles, ran our string lines and checked our measurements. This told us exactly where the brickwork would finish. We then had to dig out the earth for the concrete footings. Portlands' concise plans gave us all the relevant dimensions required for the footings.

Bringing in the bricklayer Once the footings were excavated, we were ready to build the walls. We used an experienced bricklayer, Steve, to tackle the majority of the facing brickwork. To help to cut the costs down a little, Paul volunteered to labour for Steve. He stacked the bricks at handy intervals around the site for Steve's convenience. In between these piles of bricks were placed spot boards – pieces of ply used for placing the cement. It was important to keep the bricks dry when they were stacked up ready to use. Otherwise, cement absorbs the moisture from the brick and becomes more watery. It then tends to ooze down the face of the completed brickwork, making a mess. The exterior brickwork was pointed in a way to encourage rainwater to be directed away from the brick and also to match the rest of the property's pointing.

 Above Paul and Steve removing the guttering – part of the demolition work that we carried out before erecting the conservatory.

 Warning
Always bend nails over in timber to stop anyone from hurting themselves if they tread on them.

Diary
The two fitters from Portland Conservatories told us that they often received verbal abuse from neighbours, who are faced with the unappealing prospect of having an imposing conservatory roof to look at. Fortunately, our neighbours have only complimented us on how much we have improved our property.

Conservatory: what we did

Above This shows the rear of the garage after blocking up to separate the garage from the conservatory, leaving a doorway for access.

The expert at work Like the expert he is, Steve made the bricklaying look deceptively simple. He would take a brick, butter it up with cement on one end, lay a bed of cement on the previous row of bricks, place the brick firmly on the previous row (following his string line as a guide) and gently tap it into place followed by another and another until each course was completed. He made regular vertical and horizontal checks with his spirit level. The exterior brickwork was pointed in such a way as to encourage rainwater to be directed away from the brick and also to match the rest of the property's pointing.

Building the retaining walls The retaining walls were built only to damp course height. We did not build the walls all the way up for several reasons: it would have been impossible to get the concrete slab level with the walls in place; if the walls were built we would not have wanted to get concrete splashes onto the facing brickwork; and as it takes a few days for the cement to truly harden, it would have been easy to damage the strength of the new brickwork. With the retaining walls at damp-course height we mixed and poured the concrete slab, known as the base.

Preparing the base The height of the base was determined so that the finished floor height was the same as the bungalow floor height, eliminating the need for a step. After the slab was laid, we completed the walls to the heights as shown in the plans. Portland sent a team of two fitters to erect the framework onto our base, with no problems. The glass was fitted and the construction of the conservatory completed.

Erecting the conservatory Once the framework was up and the glazing in, we were able to complete the interior of the conservatory with plastering, painting, electrical fitting and carpentry jobs such as fitting the doors, skirting and laying the floor.

Expert advice

 DIY tips

To mark out the earth to be excavated for the footings, stand astride the string line looking directly down on it. Take some sand and place your hands directly above the string. Release some sand by rubbing your hands together, looking vertically down upon the string line. Walk slowly around all the string lines, releasing sand as you go. You have now marked out the perimeter of the wall area to the ground. Ideally, the footings for a conservatory should be 450mm (18in) wide by 450mm (18in) deep. While digging out, keep your trench sides as neat and vertical as possible – this will depend on the type of soil you are digging. This is important for estimating required materials. If you dig out too much you will need more concrete.

Laying the floor Originally we were going to tile the conservatory floor. However, we changed our plans and decided to fit a new wooden floor to match the new living room. Because we poured the concrete for the slab with a view to tiling the floor, we had to solve the problem of attaching wooden joists to a concrete floor, with floorboards on top to match the floor height in the bungalow. We screwed blocks of wood to the concrete floor, attached the joists to these and placed the floorboards on top of the joists. Luckily, our measurements worked out to the same height as the bungalow floor. When the floor was complete, we laid down matting from Just Flooring.

The final transformation The furniture was made to order from Lloyd Loom, and we added vibrant cushions for a touch of colour. This completed the transformation of this area from a dingy, damp end of the garage to a bright and airy conservatory that is a wonderful addition to our house.

Left Here you can see the main body of the conservatory, with wood for the floor sitting on blocks in preparation for the floorboards to be laid.

 DIY tips

Before pouring concrete into the trench for footings, make eight or so stakes about 600mm (24in) long. Drive the stakes vertically at two-metre intervals around the bottom and middle of the trench. The top of the stake will be the desired height of the concrete. This is worked out by referring to your plans. Next, place a spirit level from the first stake to the second stake and level off until all stakes are at a level height around the trench. Pour the concrete and level to these heights. You will have sufficient depth of footings to the correct height to start building up to damp course height.

Conservatory: Q and A

Q What are the pros and cons of mixing your own concrete compared with buying readymixed?

A Ready-mixed concrete is easier to use, less time-consuming but more expensive. Self-mix concrete is more cost-effective but also more labour-intensive. You also need to take into consideration the hire of a cement mixer.

Q What different types of flooring are suitable in a conservatory?

A We chose to put wooden floors down to match the lounge adjoining the conservatory so that this room flowed into the next. Also, timber is naturally a warmer product than tiles or stone. Laminate flooring is an option to be considered, but be aware that there are various grades of quality, and some are not designed to be used in areas of heavy traffic or to have water spilled on them.

Q What are good ways of heating a conservatory?

A Due to the large expanse of window area in conservatories, the temperature will behave very much like a greenhouse (even if you have double-glazed windows). Even on summer nights it can become cold inside. Therefore some form of heating is essential if you are going to get the most use out of this addition to your home. If you have gas central heating it will not take long for a competent plumber to add to the existing system already in use. They will be able to tell you whether your existing boiler will be able to cope with the need for more radiators. The pipework is best added while the base for the conservatory is being constructed. Other methods for heating the conservatory are night storage heaters. They work by using electricity to warm thermal bricks during the night when electricity is cheaper. These bricks are designed to then release the heat that was saved up when it is needed. This is achieved with the aid of vents built on the heater and enables you some kind of heat control. Underfloor heating is a good idea. Built into the floor is a network of copper pipes that extend across the whole floor area. This works like a conventional water-filled radiator system. This system is particularly good if you have a tiled or stone-floored conservatory. The drawback of this system is that it can be expensive to fix because of the pipes being set into the floor.

▶ **Right** The completed conservatory with a view out into the garden. It is spacious, light, warm and welcoming at all times of the year. We decided to have wooden floors in here rather than tiles to provide a visual link with the adjoining lounge. Timber is also warmer than tiles or stone.

Hall: introduction

Making a grand entrance with sumptuous wallpaper, ornate panelling and a salvaged staircase

 Above The hallway in the early stages of the project, with the old Artexed ceiling and before the staircase was fitted. The stepladder at the end of the corridor was the only way we could get up to the loft extension.

What we wanted to achieve The hallway is obviously the first thing that people see when they come into your house. It's an ideal opportunity to create the impression that you want people to have of you and your home, but you shouldn't go overboard. Always create an atmosphere that makes you happy and comfortable, rather than trying to impress other people. In our case, the hallway originally was dark and poky and felt cluttered. I wanted to create space, elegance and light. We also wanted to add our own unique touch by renovating salvaged items and adapting items that we found. We fitted a renovated staircase, double doors to the kitchen, found an old pew that worked really well in the space, and adapted some ornate panelling to disguise the radiator.

The structural alterations We left the decoration of the hallway until late in the project, because the building traffic coming through from one end of the house to the other meant that any work would have been damaged. We also had structural work to do before we could even think about decorating ideas. This included knocking down a 2m x 2.4m (6ft 6in x 7ft 8in) section of brick internal wall in the hallway. When we were working on the kitchen we demolished a wall between the kitchen and the smallest room in the house. This enabled us to extend the kitchen and allowed for stair access into the newly converted loft. Immediately to the right of the bathroom was the original single kitchen door which we blocked up with the bricks we had set aside from a previous demolition job in the house. When the structural alterations had been made, and the principal work done in the rest of the house, we could start the hallway.

Increasing the light One of the major problems we faced in the hallway was of how to increase the natural lighting in an area that originally was very dark, as is

Expert advice

 DIY tips

When getting nails out of timber, you may find that some are too stubborn to remove. In this case, use a nail punch to push them in further and then cover the heads with putty before decorating.

 Moneysavers

If you are looking for items in salvage yards, you will probably find that items that have been cleaned up already are a lot more expensive than items that you need to restore yourself. Some yards will also let you negotiate prices on such items.

 DIY tips

When you are painting, have a small tub of water handy to keep your brushes in. This prevents them from drying out. You can do this with both oil and emulsion brushes – they can stay like this for days.

often the case in bungalows. We achieved this in three ways. First of all we fitted reclaimed Victorian pine double doors with glass panels in their top halves as the new entrance doors from the hallway to the kitchen. This let in the light from the kitchen. Secondly, we positioned a large velux window (the largest one we could obtain!) directly over the area set aside for our 'to be constructed' stairwell. Thirdly, we cleaned the glass on the front two doors!

The ceiling mouldings Locker & Riley, the plastering company, supplied the beautiful ceiling mouldings throughout the ground floor. The ceiling mouldings, with their classical, ornamental pattern, helped to inspire me with the overall look in the hallway. I wanted to carry on the elegant style with an ornate wallpaper and classical panelling. The panelling would also have a practical function, as the children tended to run along the hallway dragging their hands along the walls.

Above Here you can see the beautiful pattern of the Timney Fowler wallpaper. The pew, which sits opposite the kitchen doors, was one of my salvage bargains.

Hall: what we did

Below The view along the hallway to the bathroom, while we were replacing the flooring. Living in such mess became second nature!

Finding the staircase We are fortunate where we live because we have access to several excellent salvage reclamation yards. In one of these we found an unpromising-looking beaten-up staircase that we decided to restore. This was in March 1998, when we had been in the house for nine months. We had done the loft conversion, but could only get up to the room via a stepladder – not ideal. The staircase we found at the yard was very reasonably priced compared to others we had looked at. Paul actually pointed it out as a joke because it was in such a bad state. The colour drained from his face when I decided to buy it and he realised he would have to restore it. It was covered in tar, it was too wide, and would need to be dismantled, cut up, cleaned off and then put back together in a different shape. However, it was only a few pounds, including delivery, compared with the cost of a new staircase for several thousand pounds not including the cost of fitting.

Renovating the staircase Paul had to fit the 1.5m x 7.5m (5ft x 24ft 6in) staircase into a 2.5m (8ft) square space designed for a staircase that had to go up by six stairs, turn 180 degrees and go up a further seven steps. Paul's first job was to take off the sides, which was not an easy task. Luckily the sides weren't glued on but held together by long clasp nails that had rusted. He then had to use a sledgehammer to dismantle the stairs. The next task was to remove all the nails and the layers of old paint. Paul used an electric wood planer on the straight flat surfaces and then sanded the wood with an orbital sander. He started by using a coarse sandpaper, known as P40, and then moved on to the finer grades. The sanded-down wood revealed a beautiful grain.

Fitting the staircase When we first looked into the costs of commissioning the local joinery to build a staircase, they gave us a computerised plan with all the correct measurements. We used this plan when jigging the staircase to fit. Paul transferred the measurements to the walls and cut the reclaimed timber to suit.

Expert advice

 Feng Shui

According to Nick, our hallway was an unlucky area. He predicted that we would have conflicts, lawsuits and illness, which we have experienced in this house. He recommended decorating in greys, silvers and white. He also said we should increase the lighting in this area. This is something we intended to do anyway. Nick advised us that, as the staircase is opposite the front door, energy travels up the stairs rather than around the home. He suggested hanging a windchime at the bottom of the stairs to deflect energy around the ground floor. Nick also stressed the importance of keeping the windows clean!

The panelling idea Our next major task in the hallway was constructing the panelling. Renovations were well under way at our home while we were broadcasting it over the internet. I had approached several manufacturers of high-quality goods to sponsor us with products in return for featuring them on our live broadcasts. One of these was Timney Fowler, who provided us with fabrics and wallpapers. We thought that if the wallpaper were to go from the ceiling to the floor in this area, this luxurious paper might get damaged. This prompted the idea of the panelling. We also thought panelling would be a good way of hiding the radiator, as well as being in keeping with the elegant, neo-classical look that we were trying to achieve. We visited several stately homes in the area to get some inspiration.

Building the panelling The first stage of creating the panelling was to secure roofing battens of 19mm x 35mm (¾in x 1½in) horizontally to a height of 1m (3ft) spaced about 200mm (8in) apart down the wall. Next, we secured sheets of 8mm (½in) ply to the battens using small countersunk screws. To create the panelled look, we used PAR (planned and ready) timber of 10mm (½in) depth by 100mm (4in) wide in 5m (16ft 6in) lengths. We then chose a suitable dado thickness to run around the top of the panelling and secured skirting along the bottom using a mitre-cutting hand tool for the corners.

Finishing the panelling To finish the panelling off we fixed infill quarter round strips of wood, 10mm x 10mm (½in x ½in), to take away the squared-edge look. These strips had been detailed. We could have used a router to achieve this effect but we couldn't justify the cost of purchasing one just for one job. The detailed lengths of timber come in lengths of 2.4m (8ft) and various styles and widths from John Parr Joinery. They are sold at various DIY outlets. They are useful for hiding gaps as they bend to a tight fit and can be secured in place with products such as Gripfil or Nonails, with a few securing pins to hold them in place until the adhesive material has set.

Disguising the radiator Most houses with central heating have radiators, which are often quite unattractive. We decided to hide the hallway radiator with an old fireplace that we salvaged from a local dump, and some mahogany screens that we bought from a cheap discount store. It is important to be able to gain access to the radiator in case of leaks or other plumbing problems, so we fixed the screens with two small hinges so they could be opened like a door. Screening off the radiator not only looks effective but is heat-efficient. Many people have remarked on how the top of the fireplace seems to throw the heat into the middle of the hallway instead of just heating the ceiling.

Below The doors that were salvaged from an old nunnery. We hung these between the hallway and the kitchen.

Hall: what we did

Chasing in the cables When the rest of the house was rewired, the electric cables to the hallway were left dangling through the ceiling, so our next step was to chase them in. This means hiding cables in the wall out of sight. The idea is to remove as little plaster as possible, so you can repair the damage more easily. Be sure to mark the correct height of the wall lights. Draw two parallel lines about 60mm (2in) apart down the wall. Remove the plaster from the brickwork by using a bolster. Do not hammer away in just one place, otherwise you will remove too much plaster. Firmly tap along the marked lines, with one good hit of the bolster, and then move it along to the next part until you have made a slight indentation all the way along the marked lines. Now you can start hitting with a bit more vigour. You should find that only the area where the cables are going will be removed. Place the cables under a hard plastic trunking strip specially designed to protect the wiring, and secure it in place using a small nail. Once you have done this you can apply the undercoat plaster and plaster smooth using multifinish.

Above When we first saw this staircase in the salvage reclamation yard it was one foot too wide for the space we needed, covered in tar, extremely battered, full of old rusty nails and depressing to look at. It was a satisfying challenge to transform it.

Opposite We decided to hide our radiators by using a combination of an old fireplace that came from a local dump and some mahogany screens that we brought from a discount store.

Final tasks First, we stripped the floor back to a clean finish, ready to be varnished. Next, we applied matt emulsion on the ceiling in colours to match the background of the paper. We prepared and painted the panelling and the door frames with the same shade of paint, but using an oil-based satin finish. Once the painting had been completed in this area we could think about hanging the wallpaper. First of all we decided to hang lining paper because the walls were rather rough. Lining paper helps to smooth out undulations on the wall and gives a solid surface on which to hang a quality wallpaper. Our electrician also connected the wall lights, which were supplied from Endon Lighting. I didn't want the hallway to be littered with the usual mess that collects in hallways such as people's coats, shoes and bags. We built a cupboard under the stairs for storage instead. We also have the utility room next to the kitchen for such items.

Expert advice

Diary

We left the decoration of the hallway until last, mainly because of the building traffic coming through from one end of the house to the other.

DIY tips

When hitting any wood with a hammer, avoid damaging it by placing another piece of wood against it and hitting that. Otherwise you will end up with 'half moons' – semi-circular indentations that are impossible to remove.

Moneysavers

We chose salvaged ornate screens to hide our radiators, but there are various types of new grills you can use to suit your budget, such as wood, plywood, MDF or hardboard.

 Warning

Always wear a dust mask when doing any sanding jobs. This will stop you breathing in wood dust and paint – old paint was formulated with lead, which is extremely poisonous.

 DIY tips

When painting it is advisable to have several sizes of brush handy, including a small brush known as a fitch, which is excellent for getting into corners. 1in, 2in, 3in, 4in (2.5, 5, 7.5 and 9cm) brushes are also useful.

 Timetable tips

The electrics were sorted after the staircase had been built and the panelling and ceiling mouldings fixed. The rest of the house had been rewired and the cables dangled through the ceiling.

Hall: the finished room

The overall effect I am very pleased with the way the hallway works as the entrance to our 'kingdom'. I think we have created the elegant and graceful atmosphere that we wanted to achieve. The main colour in this area is grey, which is a pleasingly neutral colour as well as being authentically classical.

The wallpaper The wallpaper that we chose was from Timney Fowler's 'Passage in Time' collection. This is decorated with cherubs, urns and gothic faces, – ideal for a classical look. This luxurious paper is handprinted, which made it particularly difficult to hang, because the variations in the pattern made the edges hard to match. The wallpaper prints are not too big, fussy or overbearing for our relatively narrow hallway. The pattern also ties in beautifully with the linear pattern of the panelling and the pew.

Right The salvaged staircase in its finished glory. They even creak, which some people might find annoying, but I think helps to create the atmosphere of being in a country cottage rather than a fifty-year-old bungalow.

Opposite The finished effect – this is the view along the hallway towards the front door. The hallway is light, uncluttered and elegant, and makes a fitting entranceway to our home.

Hall: questions and answers

Q What are important things to remember when planning a hallway?

A Your hallway is the highway into your home. It is the introduction room for your guests. Try not to clutter this part of your house. There is nothing worse than getting in from a hard day's work and tripping over the coatstand and then a chair and knocking lots of ornaments off the hall table as you catch your balance.

Q What sort of flooring might be most effective in a hallway?

A I favour using rugs over hardwood floors as hallways are heavy-traffic areas and therefore tend to get dirty very quickly. Rugs can easily be rolled up and cleaned outside. Hard floors are easy to sweep and are far more hygienic than carpets, particularly if you have pets. Another bonus is that you can take your rugs with you when you move. It is also less costly when you decide to redecorate. You need only buy a new hall rug rather than replacing an entire carpet with carpeting, underlay and then paying someone to fix the carpet. Using rugs also gives you far more versatility when it comes to decorating schemes. Carpet tends to be a fixture that people work around when they choose colours and schemes for their rooms, choosing their curtains and sofas to match. It seems silly to go to such lengths to make a room work just for the sake of a carpet. Also, the fewer things you have fixed in rooms, the more you can move them around the home.

Q What are some good ideas for wallcoverings in hallways?

A Panelling is great for hallways. Kids tend to use walls to balance. I often used to see my children with their arms out like aeroplane wings, gliding down the hallway and wiping their grubby hands on the walls. By using

panelling you can wipe the panel without damaging the wallpaper. Unless you buy a wallpaper that is coated with a thick layer of plastic vinyl, you can easily damage the wallpaper after a few wipes with a damp cloth. You are also likely to make the pattern fade. Either painting or panelling the hallway is the easiest way to look after it. And your home should not be hard work all the time.

Q Bearing in mind that the hallway is the entrance to a home, what ways are there to increase security and deter burglars?

A I always hang full-length curtains next to my front door in the hallway. This is mainly for security reasons, but it also has the added bonus of helping to keep out draughts. Many people have glass in their doors and at night you can easily be watched from the outside as you walk around in your rooms. There are several other methods you can use:

- Leave a pair of shoes by the inside of the door when you go out, because it looks as if there could be someone at home.

- We tend to leave a television on when we go out rather than just a light. A television gives off flickers of movement and creates shadows and noise. In a lit-up room it is soon easy to tell whether there is really anyone there.

- Beware of the dog signs are also a good tip. It doesn't matter whether you actually have a dog or not, but it might be enough to deter a potential burglar who won't hang around long enough to check whether your pet exists.

- We have motion-sensitive security lights outside. The cats are great because they are always setting these off when we are out.

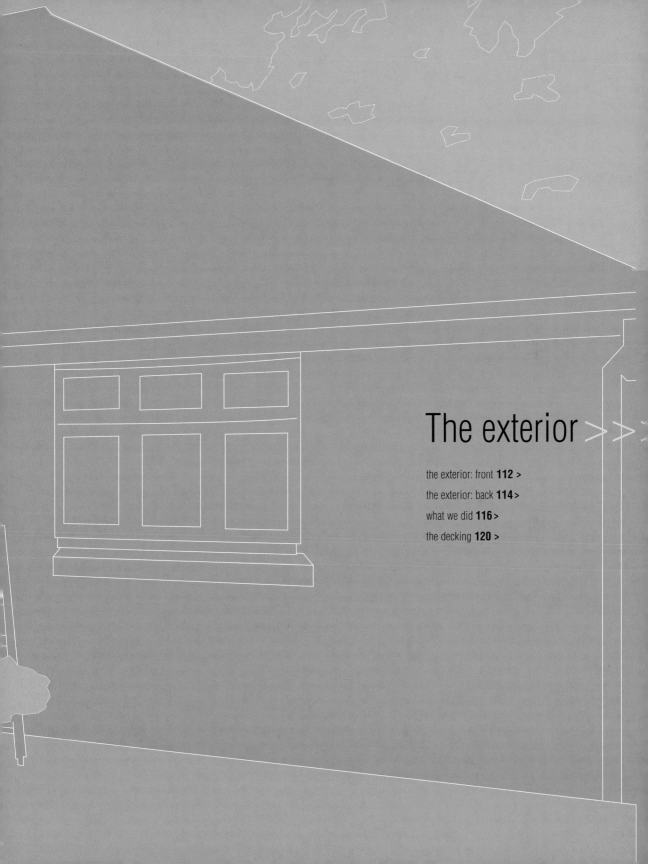

The exterior >>>

The exterior: front

We made the front of our property smart and stylish with timber decking and steps up to the front door, and stone chippings in the driveway

First impressions My first impressions of the front of the house were the horrible blue-painted windows, the old rotting drainpipes, and the uneven concrete path we walked on to get to the front door. The bumpy front lawn was a slushy mush because it had been raining, which made me think that the front garden would be no good to us and the children in poor weather. There were sliding doors attached to the brickwork in front of the main house doors to create a porch, and this seemed annoying. Transforming the front of the house was one of my main projects. Many people tend to use the front of the house just for parking. This seems to me a waste of land. Fitting the decking at the front of the house created a wonderful sun trap for us to relax outside. The driveway still had ample parking for four cars. We also allowed space for trees and bushes.

Expert advice

 Moneysavers

We saved money by building up our new driveway using discarded hardcore from our demolition work. This also saved us money on skips. However, the downside to this was that for a very long time our driveway was unusable and looked like a bomb site – or so the children kept getting told at school!

 Diary

When we built the decking at the front, we also got planning permission to raise the height of the wall so that people could not see in when they drove past. This gave us more privacy.

the exterior

The exterior: back

The back of our house was transformed by a cottage-style back door, the conservatory and the timber decking leading out to the garden

The back of the house The main improvement to the back of the house was the addition of the conservatory. We also built timber decking out here rather than having a conventional stone-flagged patio. There had been a back door on the west side of the house that led from the kitchen out to a small lean-to porch, and sliding patio doors from the bedroom next to the kitchen. We blocked up the old kitchen door, knocked down the

porch and replaced the patio doors with a reclaimed cottage-style wooden door when we constructed the new utility room. There was also a shed in the back garden that had a toilet in it. This was right outside the kitchen window. I remember thinking what a shame it was to spoil the view of the garden – although admittedly there wasn't a lot to look at originally – just a wide expanse of grass and a few neglected shrubs.

Expert advice

 Feng Shui

Nick said that the main entrance to our house faces south, which represents fame and recognition – striking when you consider all the media attention that we and our house have received. However, he said that this area is also connected with illness, and Paul and I have had health problems in the last year. Nick said that plants placed beside the front door would help to balance the good energy. He also said that the wooden steps up to the front door tended to slow energy too much and suggested that placing plants by the door would help to lift the energy up the steps. He also said it was important to keep the glass in the doors clean at all times.

The exterior: what we did

 Above Working on the construction of the conservatory, under the eyes of the documentary film crew.

What we were faced with When we first moved in, the exterior of the property was not particularly appealing. The first thing you saw on approaching the house was a 1.8m/6ft-high retaining wall with rusted wrought-iron gates that only allowed a single vehicle onto the concrete driveway that led to the front of the garage. The wall only went along the front boundary of our property between us and the public highway and was loose in places. On the western boundary of our home was a hedge consisting of 2.4m/8ft-high fir trees that finished at the front of the bungalow and urgently needed clipping. From the fir trees to the back of the house, our boundary consisted of a wall of concrete blocks, which was loose, unsightly and potentially dangerous. To the east was a small retaining wall with shrubs on our side. The eastern wall belonged to the neighbour on that side and therefore we couldn't do anything to it. This wall enclosed a small lawn that became waterlogged whenever it rained. The northern boundary, which backed onto farm land, consisted of mature and very spiky blackberry

Expert advice

📖 Diary

When we were clearing the ground in the back garden, we hired a mechanical digger for the weekend to remove the topsoil. We then piled this up in one corner of the front garden. Paul is fortunate to have

relatives who are farmers, who came along and loaded up some 18 tonnes of this topsoil and dumped it in a corner of one their fields. Paul returned the favour by doing some decorating free of charge.

 ### DIY tips

When you are doing a lot of clearing and demolition work, you need to dispose of your rubbish and rubble safely. Hiring a skip is generally the best solution.

bushes, about 16m (52ft) wide. On the east side of the property, which is our neighbours' responsibility, is a shiplap-panelled fence.

The driveway and approach Originally, on approaching the property you would drive up the ugly concrete driveway and step onto the rough-looking lawn that became extremely muddy in the winter season. You would then have to negotiate steps of several sizes and different types of materials before reaching the front door. There was a brick step, then a tile step, then some concrete. Nothing matched and it all looked very unattractive.

The work we undertook It is easier to say what we intended to keep than to say what we intended to change. We did not touch any of the eastern boundary and we left the mature hedging in the rear garden on the west side. Apart from that, everything changed.

Below Paul working on the new back door. We replaced old patio sliding doors with a reclaimed wooded cottage-style door leading from the utility room out to the garden.

The driveway We knocked down the boundary walls with a sledgehammer. We used the material as hardcore to put on the driveway at the front of the house. The front garden was always boggy, so putting our building rubble there was a way of building up the ground level and improving the drainage. Once the whole ground area had been covered by a layer of bricks and blocks, another layer of hard core was laid on top. This gave the driveway a firm base to support our vehicles.

Clearing the ground We dug up the ground in the rear garden, ready for it to be landscaped and planted. All vegetation, including the boundary of fir trees, was removed from the front of the property with a mechanical digger.

Left Paul and our builder Steve replacing fascias. We removed the old metal ones, which were decaying, and replaced them with plastic ones that are easier to maintain.

The exterior: what we did

The roof When we tackled the exterior of the bungalow itself, the first job we looked at was the roof. Fortunately, the roof was sound. The only work we did to it was to build a pitched canopy above the garage parapet wall. We did this with tiles to match the roof on the bungalow and the other side of the front of the bungalow, which had been extended and tiled on the roof. The canopy was built on the same principles as a pitched roof, using tiles that had been saved from where we had installed velux windows into the roof and so matched the roof exactly. We built the canopy purely for aesthetic reasons. It gives the appearance that the bungalow is wider, which it is due to the conservatory at the back of the garage.

The fascias The next stage of work was to look at the fascias, which hold the guttering. These places tend to be problem areas for decay because of water ingress. Although our fascias were not decayed, they had over the years been

Below Steve filling in a window. He had to do this by cutting away some of the good bricks so that he could blend the bricks in and fill in the hole in as if it was never there.

Below right When we were working on the conservatory we had to move the contents of the garage outside for temporary storage space.

Expert advice

 Planning tips

Fences and walls do not need planning permission provided that no part of the fence or wall is higher than 1m (3ft) where it runs along the boundary between a house and road. In other parts of the garden, a fence or wall may be 2m (6ft) high as long as it does not obscure a motorist's view from a road. Other restrictions regarding fences and walls may affect your home – for example you may need to obtain planning permission on an open-plan estate.

 DIY tips

Electric cables or water pipes could pose a problem if you are doing demolition work. There is equipment you can buy or hire that detects wires and cables so check before you get the sledgehammer out.

given many coats of paint and would require as many coats again in the future to keep them looking in good condition. We decided to replace the fascias, guttering, downpipes and soffits (under surfaces of the lintels) with new plastic types, so that in the future these areas would only require a quick wipe over. Only basic carpentry skills were required to attach the plastic fittings to the house. We left the old timber in place but removed the old cast-iron rainwater fittings. The new plastic fascias and soffits were placed on top of the old timber, then screwed and nailed into place.

The exterior woodwork and windows All the exterior woodwork was painted a light blue and hadn't been touched for five years. It was peeling in places, especially on the window sills and needed urgent attention to prevent the wood from rotting. The windows were of an original leaded light design, with individual cut pieces of glass between the lead. We stripped the paintwork off to check the condition of the bare wood. The wood appeared solid, with none of the soft patches that denote wood rot. We applied an oil-based wood primer to the exposed timber. Then we applied two undercoats and one layer of gloss to protect the timber from the weather. The doors on the exterior were in a good condition and so only required a rub down, a couple of undercoats of white to cover the blue and one gloss coat to finish.

Improving security We also looked at ways of making our home more secure. We made the front access to the property secure with the aid of new gates and a new wall that went from the front entrance to the front of bungalow. These are locked at night. Installing a new 2.1m/7ft-high fence (the maximum height permitted) between us and our neighbours on the west side made a driveway large enough to accommodate four cars. We installed movement-activated exterior lighting, because of the lack of street lighting in our road. We also put down a gravel driveway that crunches when people walk on it.

Below The bay windows at the front of the house. The entrance is made more attractive by placing pot plants either side of the front door.

Bottom A close up of the traditional lead glass that we placed in all of the windows.

 Planning tips
The driveway at the front of the house became the dumping ground for all our rubble. Although it made the front of the house look like a disaster area, it was a blessing in some ways. With any refurbishment project you always require an area for the messy jobs, such as mixing cement and plaster. This area would eventually be covered by Purbeck stone chippings.

 Warning
Paint stripping should be done in an area where there is a good flow of fresh air. Obviously this isn't a problem if you're stripping paint from exterior woodwork! Protect your hands and face, as the solution is corrosive.

the exterior

The decking

Our inspiration We were inspired to attach an American-style timber porch to our bungalow after seeing one in an American film. We specifically chose to have timber instead of a standard patio because of how lovely and warm it is to walk on or sit out on in the summer. We have decking at both the front and the back of the house.

Choosing the timber The timber we opted for was a Grade 1 Southern Yellow Pine, which is the hardest and strongest pine in the world. This is treated timber, guaranteed for forty years against rot and insect decay. It is supplied by Cox Lumber Co in the USA and comes from sustainable forests. The timber is grown in a temperate climate, which makes it particularly suitable for the UK. The timber's natural honey colour gradually weathers and bleaches to a soft silver-grey. This warm tone blends beautifully with plants and trees, and also complements gravel, natural stone and pebbles.

Choosing the company There were several reasons why we bought our timber from Cox Lumber. Their products are environmentally sound and good quality – the timber is treated in order to reduce twisting and warping; it is light in weight and easy to handle; and has good nail-holding power. It also could be stained and varnished straightaway.

Durability of the decking Once installed, the timber deck materials required little maintenance because the timber is pressure-treated to 99 per cent saturation. Once timber is felled and graded, Cox Lumber leave it to dry out naturally for two years before it is cut. This gives it extra durability. We built the decking with stainless-steel nails, screws and bolts, which will not rust.

 Top The decking at the back of the house makes the perfect place for a civilised lunch on a warm summer's day.

Above The decking and steps at the front of the house, which make for a striking and stylish entranceway.

 Right A view of the decking at the back of house, looking towards the conservatory and leading on to our landscaped garden.

Expert advice

📖 Diary

We built the deck a few years ago, before decking had become so massively popular as a patio replacement product. There were two car accidents outside our house caused by drivers rubbernecking as they went past and about twenty people stopped and knocked on the door to ask to have a closer look.

☠ Warning

If you are thinking of having timber decking, make sure that the treatment has penetrated right through the wood. Otherwise, when you knock nails in, the timber will decay from the inside.

 Warning

Check carefully when purchasing timber, particularly when buying treated timber. When timber is properly treated, it means that the wood fibres are saturated with water. As the wood dries, it shrinks. The place for timber shrinkage to occur is at the treatment plant under controlled conditions, not after the wood has been erected in a structure. Ask if the timber is guaranteed in the ground. It is also wise to ask to have a timber section sliced off to see how far the treatment has penetrated.

 Diary

The decking drew our entire family outside. We are often to be seen reading our Sunday papers out on the deck, like lazy cats basking in the sun. It is just wonderful.

The garden >>>

The garden: before

Our garden was large but almost featureless, with fence-to-fence grass and a handful of scrappy shrubs – transforming it was quite a challenge

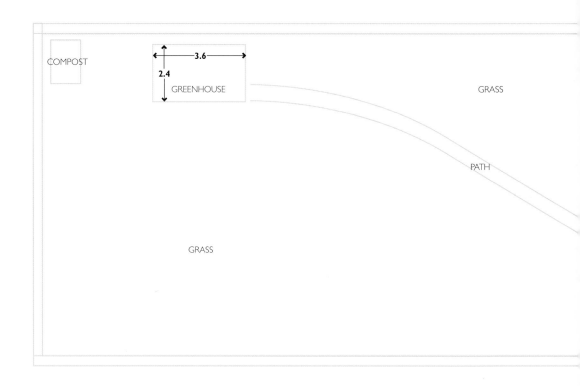

COMPOST

2.4 ←——3.6——→

GREENHOUSE

GRASS

PATH

GRASS

Measurements in metres

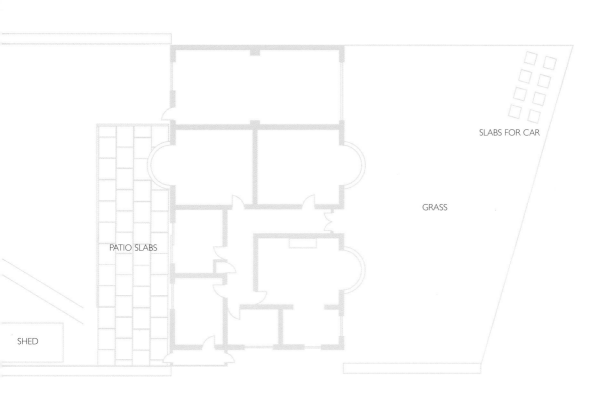

SLABS FOR CAR

GRASS

PATIO SLABS

SHED

Above The existing garden had a gentle running level, falling approximately one square metre (3ft) downhill towards the back of the bungalow. This was an excellent attribute for a display garden because whatever was created there could be viewed easily from the house – like a stage set in a theatre.

The garden: after

We wanted our garden to include areas for us to relax in, beautiful water features, interesting planting and somewhere for the children to play

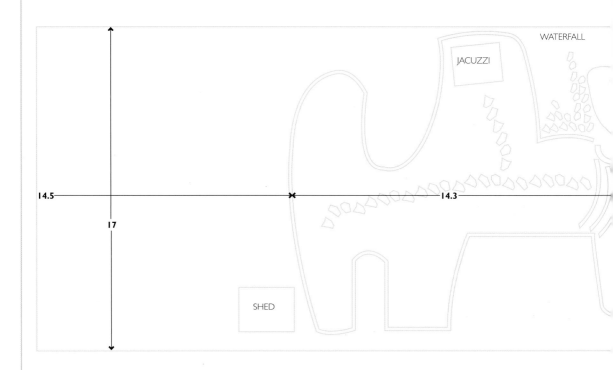

Measurements in metres

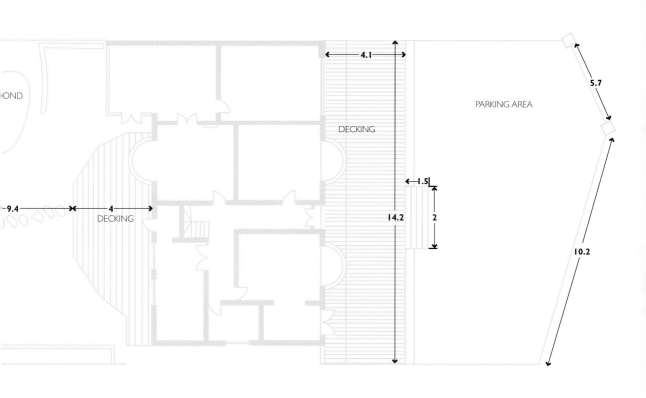

OND

PARKING AREA

DECKING

4.1

5.7

1.5

14.2

2

-9.4

4

DECKING

10.2

▲ **Above** The main features to be included
in the garden were: a timber-decked patio,
a pond, rock garden and waterfall, Jacuzzi,
heather and dwarf conifer bed, shrub
beds, dry stone wall, lawn, large stone
chipping area with stepping stone
pathways, and a shed – all in conjunction
with best garden design practices and the
advice of the Feng Shui expert.

The garden: what we did

Getting started We wanted to have the garden completed in 24 days, in time for our grand finale and party. Luckily, we had the expert help of landscape gardener Martin Catford. Our first task was dictated by the fact that we would have a hired mechanical digger for only a few days, so thinking time was limited. We used the digger to roughly mark out the garden's main features – the Jacuzzi and the pond and the changes in the height of the garden. We lowered the level of the third of the garden nearest to the house in preparation for laying stone chippings as an extension to the decking, and transferred the soil to the upper garden, where the dry stone wall was to be built. The digger achieved this work very quickly and lifted everybody's spirits because the work was underway.

Excavations and ground clearing The next stage involved digging and clearing in preparation for the main features. We started digging the pond and laid the butyl rubber sheet for the pond lining. We excavated the shallow footings for the dry-stone walling. We dug narrow slit trenches for the laying of electric armoured cables to serve the garden lighting, pond pump and waterfall, and the

Below The view of the garden from the bungalow. In the distance can be seen the hill, thought to be an ancient burial mound, that caused major Feng Shui problems later on in the project (see p.134).

Expert advice

Timesavers

Mechanical excavators are easy to use, given a few minutes' practice. They are not expensive to hire and are a real timesaver. There also is a real satisfaction in being able to move huge heaps of soil using only finger pressure.

Diary

On the night that the field hedge across the end of the garden was removed, a fearsome row broke out in the bungalow, two cats arched their backs exchanging hisses and objects were mysteriously flung across the kitchen. The children and I left to sleep in the caravan.

Paul left and chose to cycle all night long – instantly feeling better from being away from the property. It was evident that things were not right – but what, and why? Our Feng Shui expert had an explanation (see p.134).

special heavy-duty cable for the Jacuzzi. We then cleared unwanted shrubs, bramble and other waste plants, including the field boundary hedge at the far end of the garden. We wanted to extend the view of the garden out into the rounded green hill beyond – a worthy aim, but one that spelt trouble later on!

Stones and soil The next task was to visit quarries to select Purbeck stone for the rock garden, dry-stone walling, stepping-stone paving and crazy paving steps. We also had 10 tonnes (10 ton) of screened topsoil delivered. With the soil and the stones on site, the garden staff had something to tackle. The project's stonemason, Steve Dalison, began the foundations for the building of the dry-stone walls, each about 400mm (16in) wide and 450mm (18in) high, with the left-hand wall reducing to nothing to match the contours of the garden.

Selecting plants We escaped to a local nursery to select plants. It was bliss to see acres of multi-coloured carpets of heathers laid out for us to choose plants for our heather and dwarf conifer beds. We chose ones with contrasting coloured foliage and flowering times, to create interest for all seasons. The next port of call was a local garden centre in Dorset, where we were wooed by a colourful jungle of exquisite plants. We needed shrubs of all sizes for foliage, form and colour. Colourful foliage plants can look stunning for between 26 and 52 weeks a year, and if they flower too, it's a bonus. We required specimens for the main borders and to screen out the bare fence lines. We were advised not to select only deciduous shrubs, or the garden would appear dull and lifeless in the winter. A good balance is half deciduous and half evergreen. We chose dwarf conifers for the heather and alpine beds, some seasonal bedding, aquatic plants for the pool, ferns for the watercourse, specimen palms for the gravel areas, alpines for the rock garden, and good-quality tree and shrub planting compost to aid their establishment. We also bought accessories such as cobbles and feature rocks.

Below The garden in its raw state looking towards the bungalow. Knowing where to start was a real challenge – like an artist in front of a fresh white canvas.

The garden: what we did

The waterfall Work continued on the construction of the rock garden, water course and pond. The construction of the waterfall was a difficult landscaping operation. Waterfalls form a natural cleft in a hillside. Creating manmade waterfalls is therefore quite tricky; by the time the valley of 'shelves' and steps are clad in mortar, covered in butyl liner, with rocks and bedding slabs fixed into position, the overall height of the finished water course is likely to be higher than the surrounding rock garden. This can look unnatural. Quantities of pebbles were reserved for the water course, and this helped to transform it from a stark 'flight of steps' to a natural-looking mountain cascade. For further realism, we introduced a jar full of polished white 'wet-stones', designed to give the appearance of water even when there was none flowing. These were carefully placed down the centre (likely to be the wettest) part of the watercourse.

The pond By now, the pond had been dug and lined, and was filled with water. The size of the hole that was dug for the pond prompted a lot of sarcastic comments, such as 'are you going to keep alligators in that?' However, Martin calmly explained that any pond needs to be dug out considerably larger than expected. Thankfully there were no leaks when the water was put in. We could then go to town on dressing the surrounds with rounded pebbles, and with planting the margins. The cobbles were washed and placed in a wide band, about 1m (3ft) either side of the waterline. Those in the water gave the impression that the pebbles went all the way into the pool, while those emerging from the water were blended with a careful scattering of small pebbles so as to create a fading-off unification with the surrounding Purbeck chippings. The finished effect was most successful. The pebbled beach effect is also safer than a pond with a ledge, particularly with children around. You can't just trip over and fall in because the pond deepens gradually.

The heather bed The heather bed was shaped, raked, profiled to perfection and made ready for planting. We added a little visual interest by using pieces of Purbeck rock in three rows (two of three and one of two). These were designed to hold back some of the soil and thereby accentuate the difference in height between the lower soil in front of each rock and the higher behind. This meant that the heather bed would have a natural undulation and be more pleasing to the eye. Eleven boxes, each containing twenty heathers were planted and dusted with Irish moss peat. A lay-flat sprayline hosepipe was carefully laid across to deliver a fine mist spray. When the heather bed was finished, it seemed like a good time to define other planting areas so that edging stones could be mortared into position. Meanwhile, we had to frequently water the unplanted shrubs, as the weather was dry and hot.

Above The garden lights are switched on at night to illuminate the pond, waterfall, palms and other key plants with magical precision.

Right The view of the garden towards the bungalow, with paths of chippings and Purbeck stone paving slabs flanked by colourful flower beds and two 3.5m (12ft) tall Canary Island palms.

The garden: what we did

Walls and pathways The dry-stone walling was constructed, along with a winding row of Purbeck stone edgings, along the pathways. These defined the beds and contained the limestone chippings from which the paths were built, otherwise these would migrate. Natural Purbeck stepping stones were carefully placed at a comfortable walking distance apart. These were laid dry as the surrounding chippings helped to stabilise them. Meanwhile, our daughters painted the fence with Amazonia green preservative, a natural green that is easy on the eye. While they were in the mood, the garden shed was similarly coated!

The lawn and the plants The weather became hotter still, just what we did not want for turf laying. However, we made the best of circumstances, and the laying of the lawn was completed quickly, due in part to the light nature of each turf roll. Elsewhere in the garden, the planting continued apace, and this became the biggest contribution to the transformation of the garden – it turned a building site into a colourful garden. We spread graded pine-bark mulch around most of the planting areas to assist the growth of the plants. Numerous glazed flower pots were planted up with vibrantly coloured Impatiens 'New Guinea Hybrids', and posted around the outside of the upper Purbeck stone-chipping areas. Some late adjustments were made to the pond planting, and a few extra containers were planted up, including two massive bamboo plants that were placed either side of the Jacuzzi.

The finishing touches Further electrical connections and refinements were made to the garden lights by our electrician. We were racing to reach a deadline for the grand finale and evening party, so the final day of the project saw frenetic activity on many fronts. We hosed down the pathways and stepping stones, and raced around to tidy away tools, plant pots and debris, before the arrival of our guests and the celebration of the project's completion.

Opposite The pond and rock garden, which was built with planting pockets in sheltered corners that we crammed with hardy ferns. The effect is that of a Highland stream.

Below The natural, subtle colours of the pebbles and stones are beautiful in themselves and make a wonderful backdrop for the plants around the pond.

Expert advice

Details

- When choosing plants, select ones with contrasting coloured foliage and flowering times. This creates interest for all seasons of the year, and produces a beautiful patchwork quilt effect.

- When planting, ensure that like-coloured foliages are kept apart, and opposites placed next to each other – i.e. greens next to yellows, yellows next to reds, and reds next to silvers. This emphasizes nature's differences.

The garden: the Feng Shui story

Finding inspiration Our garden was large, square and almost completely featureless. It wasn't particularly inspiring. Nick Sunderland, the Feng Shui consultant gave his own advice, which, I have to admit, we didn't follow very closely, but other people might find it useful!

Our Feng Shui advice Nick said that the hedging and fencing at the left should be higher than the right as you look out from the front – it is not balanced at the moment. The front should have been left open to allow energy to enter, but a wall and high gates were added, which block the energy. Nick warned us about this and said we should create a lower section of the wall facing the door to allow the energy to flow. The only compensation is that the house is slightly raised. The rear of the house faced a hedge that prevented negative yin energy from surging towards the back door. This was removed against Nick's instructions. He said we should paint the door white to help remedy this, and suggested that we replant the hedge.

The placement of the pond The water pool was calculated to be in a certain section of the garden to prevent problems. We ignored this, and put it too close to the house. Nick predicted that it would cause illness and financial obstacles for us. Problems started the day it was filled with water. One of the most important aspects of Feng Shui is that balance and harmony prevail, and Nick felt that we had failed to achieve this. However, we felt that in terms of the dimension and scale of the garden, a large waterfall cascading over rocks with lots of pebbles and plants would have the necessary visual impact, particularly when sitting in the conservatory. I had been inspired by a friend who used to live in New Zealand and had a Jacuzzi on a deck that overlooked hills and mountains. I could imagine fitting the Jacuzzi next to the top of the waterfall so I could look down over it. It wasn't quite a mountain view but it was still appealing.

Opposite The waterfall is an impressive feature of the garden, with its cascading water and dramatically placed plants. However, in Feng Shui terms, the waterfall was badly placed and predicted to cause bad luck.

Below Purbeck slabs set in Purbeck chippings. We were advised to form the path in a lazy curve to prevent the Feng Shui yang influence from reaching the house. Gentle curves also make for more interesting landscaping.

Expert advice

Feng Shui

We removed the field boundary hedge at the far end of the garden to extend the view out into the rounded green hill beyond. Nick, the Feng Shui expert, was most displeased by this action, as he said it would expose the family to the harmful 'yin' influence likely to flow unheeded down the hill and in through the kitchen door. The hill was thought to be an ancient burial mound. Nick was even more critical of the pond, which we installed in the south-eastern quarter of the garden.

Relocating the garden shed from the right to the left hand (east-facing) side of the garden was acceptable, but Nick said that it would be wise to install some white metal-work also on the left – perhaps a white metal seat.

the garden

The garden: planning your garden

Starting off In our case, planning the garden was quite a challenge because there was nothing there. In some ways this was a bonus, because it was like working with a blank canvas – we could start from scratch and stretch our imaginations, because there were no features already in the garden that we had to work around. There are many factors to consider when you plan your garden, such as what you want to use it for. If you have young children, there are safety issues to think about. This is one of the reasons why our pond has a gradual slope. Our garden is quite large, 30m by 16m (98ft by 52ft), so we had scope to design different areas for different things. There is an area for our children to play in. There is the decking for us all to sit out on summer days. The waterfall and the colourful display of plants means that we can enjoy the garden from the conservatory on cooler days. Our garden furniture and parasol are in the lower section of the garden. It's relatively shady here, so it's a pleasant place to sit and eat on baking hot summer days.

Using your space With a flat, square garden you need to get the planting balance right. Don't be too hard on yourself if there are gaps. One of the joys of gardening is that you can increase your collection year by year and modify your design. For example, there is an area at the back righthand side of the garden by the row of olive trees that we couldn't decide how to use, so we decided to leave it until inspiration struck. Another good idea for using space is to grow seasonal perennials in frost-hardy pots. You can then move these around to different areas to fill in gaps left by plants that are not in season.

Using your time With any garden, but particularly with large gardens, you have to think carefully about how much time you have to maintain it. There's no point in having a huge lawn if you are never going to have time to mow it. Our time is quite constrained, so we wanted a garden that had a lot of visual impact but that was relatively easy to maintain. This is one of the reasons why there is so

Below Louise choosing plants at the garden centre. Once you know the soil type and pH of your garden, you can choose shrubs to provide foliage, form and colour.

Expert advice

Planning tips

When digging out ponds, always make the hole larger than expected, because it is going to become filled in again – with sand lining, with a pool liner, with rocks, stone, pebbles, plants and – of course – water!

Moneysavers

When redesigning a garden, the one thing you can be sure of is the shortcomings of the existing lawn. Inevitably it has to be replaced with new turf. It is always cheaper to do this than to try to save the existing turf for re-laying. Several weeks before beginning the work, spray the entire area with Glyphosate hormone herbicide. This prevents the growth of unwanted grasses into your finished scheme. Glyphosate attacks the plant internally without harming the soil.

much Purbeck stone in our garden. We used it for the rock garden, dry-stone walling, stepping-stone paving and crazy paving steps.

Above Louise heather planting, 'assisted' by three cats! Heathers are one of the types of plants that will not tolerate an alkaline soil.

Soil types Whether planning a new garden from scratch or just purchasing plants for an existing garden, one of the most important considerations is the type of soil in which your plants will be grown. The depth, texture and chemical composition of the soil determines whether the plants you select will thrive or fail. There are three main types of soil: clay, sandy and loamy. Clay soils are heavy to work and frequently waterlogged. Sandy soils tend to be too free-draining with nutrients quickly being washed out and the acidity of the soil increasing. Loamy soils are a balance of clay, sand and humus (rotted-down vegetable matter). The higher the proportion of humus, the more naturally fertile the soil.

Soil pH The pH scale defines how acid or alkaline a soil is. A neutral soil has a pH of 7.0. Anything below 6.0 is regarded as acid soil. At this level of acidity the only plants likely to thrive are rhododendrons and heathers. A pH of 8.0 and above is very alkaline, and will support hardly any plants. Soil-testing kits are available from most garden centres. Once you have determined the pH value of your soil, you can decide what plants to choose. It is best to select plants that thrive in the soil you have, but you can alter the pH to give you a wider choice.

Putting your plans into action If you are doing extensive landscaping, as we did, you need to think about how to coordinate the hire of machinery, the delivery of materials, the storage of materials and hiring any labourers. We had huge quantities of materials to work with – 20 tonnes of screened top soil, 18 tonnes of Purbeck stone chippings, 6 tonnes of wood bark, 8 tonnes of Purbeck stone walling and 6 pallets of grass turf for the new lawn. Luckily we had the large area at the front of the house to deposit these materials until we needed them.

Time management We had an artificial deadline imposed on us because of the filming of the documentary. However, even in normal circumstances there are things you need to think about. The weather can cause unscheduled problems, for example. We were very lucky to have a run of fine dry weather, with the exception of one afternoon of rain, which caused an unscheduled mess and forced us to stop work until the next morning.

 Right Early excavations in the project. It is a good idea to mark out the features that are to be most dominant to help you plan the work. Use trickles of builders' sand or the sharp corner of a spade.

Expert advice

Moneysavers

Screened topsoil is the mainstay of garden making. It is relatively inexpensive when ordering in full lorry loads. It has many uses; we needed it for the mortar in the dry-stone wall, the foundation for the turf laying, the rock garden, the heather bed, and for the bog garden pockets in the pond.

Details

Turf should be laid on a well-prepared and level surface. Lay the peripheral turfs first to secure the outline of the lawn, like a picture frame. Water the turfs immediately after laying them, preferably with a lay-flat sprinkler hose.

Left All our plants and shrubs were dug in with high-quality compost to help them thrive. It's worth paying more for good quality materials to help establish your garden.

Below We had to lay the pond liner at an early stage of the project, before the plants arrived and before we laid the paving stones for the pathway.

Coordination of works We also had the challenge of coordinating building works and garden works. We were on a particularly tight schedule because we had to transport all the materials and the diggers for the garden through the garage before the base for the conservatory was made. Initially this was easy, but when the foundations for the conservatory were dug, we had to push loaded wheelbarrows along narrow planks over deep troughs – not an easy task!

Budgeting You can spend limitless amounts of money on your garden, so set a budget and be strict with yourself. We thought it was worth paying extra for premium materials, such as the high-quality timber for the decking, and the Purbeck stone. They have more visual impact and last longer. We also thought it was worth investing in things such as high-quality compost. All our plants were dug in with top-quality tree and shrub planting and mulching compost to ensure that they had sufficient nourishment for the year.

Warning

The laying of electric armoured cables to serve the garden lighting, pond pump and waterfall, and the special heavy-duty cable for the Jacuzzi, all had to be done at an early stage to avoid damage to landscaping and planting. We dug narrow slit trenches by hand to avoid too much disruption. Armoured cable should always be used for garden projects as it is surrounded by a hardened steel sheath, and resists accidental damage by chopping with hand tools. This cable should be inserted 450mm (18in) deep, encased in soft sand, and covered a few inches above with a special yellow polythene tape marked – 'CAUTION ELECTRICITY'.

Plant list

Garden tools used for the project

3 Wheelbarrows

1 Long-handled edging shears

3 Spades

1 Mattock

2 Forks

1 Hammer and Bolster

3 Shovels

1 Cement mixer

2 Lawn/Hay rakes

1 Builder's float

2 Seed rakes

2 Mortaring trowels

2 Hand planting trowel

1 Spirit level

1 Pair of Secateurs

Materials used for the project

27 tonnes of Purbeck chippings

22 tonnes of screened topsoil

3½ tonnes of Purbeck rock garden stone

4½ tonnes of Purbeck walling stone

2 tonnes of Purbeck crazy paving

150m of Sherborne Turf

6 cubic metres of graded pine bark

4 100l bales of Irish moss peat

600 litres of Westland Tree & Shrub Planting Compost

4 80 litre sacks of Multipurpose compost

2 50 litre sacks of Ericaceous compost

4 tonnes of builders sand

2 cwts of Portland cement

2 cwts of lime

25 25 kg sacks of 40-120mm pebbles

5 25 kg sacks of 10-30mm pebbles

12 large cobblestones

1 6m by 8.5m butyl pond lining sheet

1 100m roll of weed-barrier sheeting

10 8ft tree stakes & tree ties

2 3 metre rolls of bamboo fencing

10 salt-glazed planters

3 jars of polished ornamental stones

Plants used for the project

(Listed clockwise in approximately the correct order around the garden – common names are listed where they exist.) N.B. Some plants were kindly donated, while others were selected in a summer sale. Some seasonal bedding plants were added for their colour impact and the 'look good' factor for the benefit of the finale and the cameras.

*denotes evergreen foliage.

Lefthand shrub beds

1 *Phoenix canariensis* (small) Canary Island Palm

20 *Lavandula angustifolia* 'Hidcote' (Old English Lavender)

3 *Hosta fortunei* 'Francee' (Funkia/Plantain Lily)

2 *Fuchsia* 'Dollar Princess' (Hardy Fuchsia)

4 *Dahlia* 'Murillo'

3 *Spiraea japonica* 'Candlelight'

3 *Pieris formosa* 'Forest Flame': (Flame of the Forest)

2 *Nemesia* 'Confetti'

1 Rhododendron ctvr.

1 *Prunus laurocerasus* (Common Laurel)

6 *Euonymus fortunei radicans* 'Emerald 'n Gold'

4 *Salvia sylvestris* 'May Night': (Mainacht)

2 *Cordyline australis* (Australian Cabbage Tree)

2 *Phoenix canariensis* (giant) (Canary Island Palm) – either side of steps

3 *Ceratostigma willmotianum* (Hardy Plumbago)

5 *Gaura lindheimeri* 'Whirling Butterflies'

3 *Convolvulus cneorum*

2 *Phormium tenax* 'Purpureum' (Purple-leaved New Zealand Flax)

1 *Griselinia littoralis* 'Variegata'

2 *Choisya ternata* 'Goldfinger' (Cut-leaved Golden Mexican Orange Blossom)

3 **Pieris formosa* 'Forest Flame': Flame of the Forest

3 Dwarf Bamboos

5 **Sedum spectabile* 'Autumn Joy' (Ice Plant)

6 **Euonymus fortunei radicans* 'Emerald 'n Gold'

3 **Euonymus fortunei radicans* 'Emerald Gaiety'

3 *Trachelium caeruleum* (Blue Throatwort/ Throatwort)

2 *Spiraea* 'Anthony Waterer'

1 *Dicksonia Antarctica* (giant) (Australian Tree Fern)

1 *Dicksonia Antarctica* (small) (Australian Tree Fern)

2 *Polystichum setiferum* (Soft Shield fern)

2 *Hydrangea* 'Freudenstein PP4L' (Hydrangea)

1 **Photinia Xfraseri* 'Red Robin' (giant specimen)

1 *Lavateria thuringiaca* 'Burgundy Wine' (Shrubby Mallow)

3 **Choisya ternata* 'Goldfinger': (Golden Cut-leaved Mexican Orange Blossom)

2 *Cotinus* 'Grace' (Purple-leaved Smoke Bush)

3 *Berberis thungbergii* 'Harlequin' (red-leaved Barberry)

3 *Ceratostigma willmotianum* 'Desert Skies Palm Gold (Golden Hardy Plumbago)

6 *Agapanthus* 'Headbourne Hybrids (African Lily)

1 **Escallonia* 'Gold Brian' ("Golden-leaved Escallonia")

1 *Catalpa bignonioides* 'Aurea' [std.](Golden Indian Bean Tree)

3 *auricomis* (Dwarf Bamboo)

3 **Salvia* 'Maraschino' (ornamental Sage)

2 *Lavendula stoechas* (French Lavender)

1 *Lavateria thuringiaca* 'Burgundy Wine' (Shrubby Mallow)

1 **Elaeagnus X ebbingei* 'Limelight'

Around shed borders:

2 *Clematis* 'Richard Pennell'

1 *Phormium tenax* 'Purpureum' (Purple-leaved New Zealand Flax)

3 **Lavendula multifida* 'Blue Wonder' (Mediterranean Lavender)

2 **Euonymus fortunei radicans* 'Emerald 'n Gold'

1 *Ficus carica* 'Pendula' (Weeping Fig)

3 *Lavateria thuringiaca* 'Burgundy Wine' (Pink Shrubby Mallow)

1 *Lavateria thuringiaca* 'Memories' (White Shrubby Mallow)

2 **Euonymus fortunei radicans* 'Emerald Gaiety'

Olive grove & fruit orchard:

1 *Ficus carica* 'Pendula' (Weeping Fig)

4 *Olea europaea* (European olive)

1 *Cydonia oblonga* (Quince)

2 *Prunus spp.* (Cherry)

5 *Prunus persica nectarina* (Nectarine)

Rear righthand fence boundary and nearby areas:

5 *Prunus laurocerasus* (Common Laurel)

2 *Ficus carica* (Common Fig)

1 *Wisteria sinensis* (Chinese Wisteria)

1 *Clematis* 'Prince Charles'

2 *Photinia X fraseri* 'Red Robin' [giant specimens]

1 *Rosmarinus officinalis* (Common Rosemary)

3 *Clematis* 'Prince Charles'

1 *Elaeagnus pungens* 'Maculata' [giant specimen]

1 *Clematis* 'Niobe'

1 *Hebe ctvr.* (Shrubby Veronica)

2 *Griselinia littoralis*

1 *Erica arborea* (Tree Heath)

1 *Erica arborea* 'Aurea' (Golden Tree Heath)

1 *Mahonia* 'Charity'

7 *Agapanthus* 'Headbourne Hybrids (African Lily)

2 *Phyllostachys* 'Aurea' [giant] (Fishpole Bamboo)

Heather bed:

20 *Daoecia X scotia* 'Jack Drake'

1 *Juniperus squamata* 'Blue Star'

20 *Calluna vulgaris* 'Cottswood Gold'

20 *Calluna vulgaris* 'Grey Carpet'

1 *Chamaecyparis obtusa nana* 'Gracilis'

20 *Erica carnea* 'Foxhollow'

20 *Calluna vulgaris* 'Joy Vanstone'

20 *Calluna vulgaris* 'Beoley Silver'

20 *Erica vagans* 'Kevernensis Alba'

1 *Taxus baccata* 'Fastigiata Aurea'

1 *Chamaecyparis obtusa* 'Minima Aurea'

20 *Erica carnea* 'Pink Spangles'

20 *Calluna vulgaris* 'Winter Fire'

In gravel in front of Jacuzzi:

11 *Thymus X* (Doone Valley Thyme)

8 *Thymus serpyllum* (Creeping Thyme)

4 *Thymus citriodorus* (Lemon Thyme)

Rock garden:

3 *Acorus gramineus* 'Ogan' (ornamental Sedge)

3 *Festuca glauca* 'Eliagha Blue' (Blue Fescue)

1 *Cordyline australis* 'Purpurea' (Purple-leaved Australian Cabbage Tree)

1 *Juniperus squamata* 'Blue Star'

4 *Sedum* 'Cape Bianco'

6 *Sempervivum mxd.*

3 *Saxifraga moschata* 'Cloth of Gold' (Golden Musky Saxifrage)

3 *Helianthemum* 'Wisley Primrose' (Rock Rose)

3 *Verbascum letitia* (Rock Mullein)

1 *Juniperus communis* 'Compressa' (Noah's Arc Juniper)

3 *Scutellaria orientalis* (Oriental Skullcap)

2 *Sisyrinchium californicum* 'Brachypus' (Californian Satin Flower)

3 *Thymus citriodorus* 'Variegatus' (Lemon Variegated Thyme)

5 *Cerastium tomentosum* (Snow-in-Summer/ Dusty Miller)

4 *Cotula hispanica* (Spanish Brass Buttons)

3 *Campanula carpatica* 'White Clips' (Carpathian Harebell)

3 *Campanula poschorskyana* (Dwarf Blue Harebell)

1 *Juniperus communis* 'Compressa' (Noah's Arc Juniper)

1 *Trachycarpus fortunei* (Chusan Palm)

2 *Thymus vulgaris* 'Silver Posie' (Silver-leaved Common Thyme)

3 *Geranium* 'Pink Spice' (Alpine Geranium)

1 *Acer palmatum* 'Atropurpureum' (Red-leaved Japanese Maple)

3 *Euonymus fortunei radicans* 'Emerald 'n Gold'

2 *Phyllostachys* (Dwarf Golden-leaved Bamboo)

1 **Euonymus fortunei* 'Harlequin'

1 **Cordyline australis* 'Purpurea' (Purple-leaved Australian Cabbage Tree)

4 *Diascia* 'Blackthorn Apricot'

3 *Silene uniflora* 'Druetts Variegated' (Catchfly)

3 **Cerastium tomentosum* (Snow-in-Summer/ Dusty Miller)

1 **Juniperus communis* 'Compressa' (Noah's Arc Juniper)

4 *Diascia* 'Twinkle'

3 **Helianthemum* 'Salmon Queen(Rock Rose)

3 *Silene acaulis pendunculata* 'MT Snowdon's Form' (Moss Campion)

4 **Sedum* 'Cape Bianco'

5 *Scutellaria orientalis* (Oriental skullcap)

Rear of rock garden and along eastern boundary:

3 *Hydrangea* 'Goliath'

2 *Hydrangea* 'Madame E Mouillere'

4 *Impatiens* 'New Guinea Hybrids' (Busy Lizzie)

4 *Nemesia* 'Confetti'

3 **Heucherella* 'Quicksilver'

2 *Lavandula stoechas* (French Lavender)

3 **Euonymus fortunei radicans* 'Emerald 'n Gold'

Feature planting in gravel at base of steps:

3 *Verbascum bombyciferum* 'Arctic Summer' (Mullein)

Watercourse surrounds:

4 *Polystichum acrostichoides* (Christmas Fern)

4 *Polystichum setiferum* (Soft Shield Fern)

2 *Dryopteris offinis cristata* 'The King' (Woodfern)

1 **Acorus calamus* 'Variegatus' (Myrtle Flag/M.Grass/ M. Sedge/Sweet Cane)

In or around pond margins:

6 *Lobelia cardinalis* (Cardinal Flower/Scarlet Flower)

4 *Polystichum acrostichoides* (Christmas Fern)

2 *Gunnera manicata* (Chilean Rhubarb/Prickly Rhubarb)

1 × *Hosta fortunei* 'Aureomarginata' (Funkia/Plantain Lily)

6 × *Lobelia verdarensis*

1 × *Glyceria maxima* 'Variegata', ("Reed Sweet Grass")

3 × *Geum* 'Lady Stratheden' (ornamental "Water Avens")

1 × *Caltha palustris* ("Kingcup"/"Marsh Marigold"/"Molly Blobs"/"Water Cowslip")

6 × *Primula Vialii*

6 × **Acorus calamus* 'Variegatus' ("Myrtle Flag"/"M.Grass"/"M. Sedge"/"Sweet Cane")

4 × *Houttuynia cordata* 'Chameleon'

2 × *Sagittaria* 'Flore Plena' ("Arrowhead"/"Water Archer")

2 × *Pontaderia cordata* ("Pickerel Weed")

In pond:

2 × *Nymphaea ctvrs.* ("Waterlily")

Tubs on decking:

4 *Maurandya antirrhyniflora*

4 *Impatiens* 'New Guinea Hybrids ("Busy Lizzie")

2 **Laurus nobilis* (std.) ("Bay")

2 *Cordyline australis* ("New Zealand Cabbage Trees")

4 *Hanging Baskets*

Directory

Directory

SPONSORS

The following are a selection of the companies and manufacturers who contributed to the Internet HomeMakers project:

Akzo Nobel
01480 496868

Black and Decker
0207 4133161

Brintons Carpets
www.brintons.net

Certikin International
01993 778855

Clayton Munroe
www.claytonmunroe.co.uk

Crown
01480 496868

Devises Kitchens
01380 729507

Figero Furniture
01225 815100

Forest Edge Nurseries
01202 824387

Furniture Village
01202 493100

Global Orange Groves
01202 814651

Habasco
01484 642115

Haskins Garden Centre
01202 591919

Internet Broadcasting Company
www.ibctoday.com

Keates Quarries
01929 439207

Lascos
www.lascos.co.uk

Laura Ashley
0207 8805125

Lloyd Loom Limited
01433 631566

Locker and Riley
01268 574100

Monkwell Fabrics
01202 752944

Neff
01908 328328
www.neff.co.uk

Polyvine
01454 261276

Portland Conservatories
0161 8721001

Sadolin
woodcare@stives.deconorth.com

Sandersons
01895 201530

Sony
01932 816000

The Alternative Flooring Company
0114 272 9895

Timney Fowler
0207 3516562

Tissunique
0207 3490096

Vauxhall Motors
01582 734403

ANTIQUES

The following sites are useful for buying unique antique items for your home. They are also a fun way to browse if you are looking for inspiration but can't afford the real thing.

www.antiques-domain.com

This site was developed with the aim of allowing antique dealers to market their wares to a wider audience. It contains a huge variety of items, sorted into categories such as:

- accessories
- boxes
- clocks and watches
- collectables and miscellaneous
- dolls and teddy bears
- furniture
- glass
- jewellery

www.antiquemirrorgallery.com

This is the website of a specialist antiques shop based in Kings Road, London. They are specialists in 18th- and 19th-century gilt mirrors, and also offer a restoration service. Their website contains a gallery of their current stock.

www.antiqueweb.co.uk

This website features an extensive list of contact details of antiques dealers throughout Britain, so you can find out what treasure troves are near you. Some of these dealers have their own websites.

www.antiquesworld.co.uk

This is a directory of antiques-related information, including reviews of books and magazines, lists of organisations such as collectors' clubs and dealers, and events such as antiques fairs, study courses and major exhibitions.

www.server2.grannieusedto.co.uk/home.html

This is the website of a charming, quirky Scottish antique and curios shop called Grannie Used to Have One. They have a wide range of stock including Scottish pottery, porcelain, china, glassware, brass, copper, marine items, pictures and furniture. Their web shop shows only a small sample of their range.

www.eatmyhandbagbitch.co.uk

This provocatively titled website is the homepage of a London-based shop focusing on products of post-war design, primarily Italian, Scandinavian and British items. The extremely stylish products on offer include chairs (including ones by Arne Jacobsen); desks; lights; art; and objects as diverse as salad sets, vases, record players, radios and candle holders.

www.windsorhouse.co.uk

This is the website of the Windsor House Antiques Centre, which houses 45 antique dealers. You can't order on the site, but they feature an attractive gallery so you can browse online. They deal mainly in 17th-, 18th- and 19th-century furniture, paintings, mirrors and pottery.

CONTRACTORS

The following website is a useful starting point if you want to find reliable contractors.

www.buildituk.com

This website contains an online directory of contractors. Every contractor is thoroughly screened to ensure that they hold the correct qualifications and insurance and can provide references of past works to ensure a good customer relationship record and quality of craftsmanship. The database includes details of different categories such as:

- asphalt and tarmac
- carpenters and joiners
- civil engineers
- demolition
- fencing
- flooring and tiling
- landscaping
- plastering and rendering
- scaffolding
- woodworm, dry rot and damp course specialists

You can browse the directory yourself for a contractor in your area, or you can fill in a form online describing the type of work that you need done, and the website administrators undertake to find a suitable contractor for you.

The site also contains useful information on general home maintenance, covering areas such as cupboards and shelving; flooring; home security; insulation; and general decorating.

DECKING

The following are useful websites if you want to investigate decking.

www.ajsmith.clara.net

This is the website of a timber merchants that includes a directory of UK deck builders. Many of these have websites featuring galleries of their work and price lists.

www.deckdesign.co.uk

A site with information on timber decking and non-timber decking (fibreglass and rigid PVC). This company offers a 3-D design service using computer-aided design software.

This means that you can see a simulation of what a completed deck will look like in situ.

www.directdecking.co.uk

This website includes a list of suppliers of timber decking products for the DIY builder. They are quality controlled under the ISO 9002 Quality Assurance scheme. All their timber is specifically selected for decking, and is adequately preservative treated. All the timber is sourced from selected Scandinavian joinery-grade redwood.

www.ezdeck.com

This is the website of a manufacturer of fibreglass decking. Fibreglass decking may not look as attractive as timber decking, but it is easy to install and very easy to maintain, so it is an alternative to consider. It is also considerable cheaper.

DIY

The following are useful websites for DIY tips and materials.

www.decoratingdirect.co.uk

This practical site covers cleaning products, fillers, mastics, abrasives, step ladders and tools such as brushes and scrapers. Orders of £50 and over are delivered free, and there are extensive security measures in place to protect you when ordering online.

www.diy.com

This is the website for B&Q, the DIY retailer. It is primarily an online catalogue for their range of products, encompassing tools, building and decorating materials, home furnishing products, and gardening products. You can order the products on display either online or via the telephone number given on site. Alternatively, you can just look at what they have to offer before going to your nearest store. The site also offers a number of useful features, including the facility to search for the store nearest to your home. There is a well cross-referenced section called 'B&Q Inspiration'. This is a gallery of themed rooms, along with a list of the products used to create the look. This is cross-referred to a section that tells you what tools you need to complete the job and how to do it. There also is a how-to section covering skills such as carpentry, plumbing and decorating, and an excellent reference section. This includes a feature that allows you to calculate how many boxes of tiles or rolls of wallpaper you will need to complete a project. The website also features an extensive DIY glossary, and a Buyers Guide that gives detailed and useful technical information on certain products. For example, if you look up wood-finishing products, you will get a list that covers:

• solvent-based varnish
• quick-drying varnish
• yacht or performance varnish
• floor varnish
• coloured finishes
• wood dyes
• exterior wood stains
• exterior wood preservers

You can also email a DIY query to their resident online experts, and you should usually receive a reply within 48 hours.

www.diyfixit.co.uk

This extensive website offers clear and detailed information on the most common DIY jobs. Subjects covered include carpentry, plumbing, electrics, painting, tiling, wallpapering, and central heating. The site also has a room-by-room index with a breakdown of typical jobs you would do in that room.

www.homebase.co.uk

This comprehensive site features an extensive online range of products, including:
• bathrooms and plumbing
• building and DIY equipment
• ceramic tiles and accessories
• cookshop and housewares
• curtain fitments and blinds
• decorating accessories
• flooring and rugs
• hand tools
• hardware
• lighting
• paint
• power tools
• shelving and storage
• woodcare

The site is Which? Web Trader accredited, but there is also the facility to order goods by telephone. The site also has a good inspiration section featuring rooms decorated in various styles with a certain theme, and an easy-to-follow 'how to' section if you want to try to recreate the look shown.

www.mikesart.com

This website contains many useful links to other sites, covering Home and Garden, Furniture, and Home Decor among other things. There is a glossary of design, decor and building terms for the mystified, and also a designer sketchbook, so you can try out your ideas for curtains and so on before putting them into practice.

www.repair-home.com.

This is a good general DIY site to visit if you have any questions about DIY and gardening. It's a US site, but it has useful discussion forums covering topics such as

Directory

home repairs; plumbing; heating, venting and air conditioning; gardening and landscaping; roofing; flooring; major appliances; and general tips.

FENG SHUI

The following is the website for Nick Sunderland, our Feng Shui consultant.

www.universalfengshui.com

This website provides an online Feng Shui service and also includes detailed analysis on how you can use special doors that Nick has designed for homes and offices. You will find all the information you require for a truly personalised and distinctive feng shui door that enhances your life aspirations and protects you from negative influences. If you want a direct consultation, you can call Nick on 01795 439028, email publisher@universalfengshui.com, or write to: Universal Feng Shui Ltd, 11 Sandstone Drive, Saxonfields, Sittingbourne, Kent, ME10 2PP.

FURNITURE

The following websites are a good place to start if you are looking for furniture.

www.amical-interiors.co.uk

This website features a particularly good selection of beds, in iron, oak, and pine. It also has good-quality wooden tables and dressers. This site features the latest encryption technology, so it's completely safe to place an order online.

www.athenaeumfurniture.com

This is the website for a London shop that imports high-quality Italian furniture. Their prices are competitive because they have no expensive showrooms or middle-man commissions to pay. They offer a broad range of elegant and classical furniture with sleek and simple lines, and are particularly notable for their good selection of tables.

www.conran.co.uk

This is a very stylish website from design guru Terence Conran. The online shopping catalogue is not particularly extensive, but it gives you a good feel for the type of sleek, minimalist products the Conran shops stock. These items are pretty expensive, but you have to pay for style.

www.furniture123.co.uk

This website has categories covering the living room, bedroom, dining room, music and TV units, office furniture, kitchen and garden items. The site offers you the opportunity to order free fabric samples before you commit to buying an item such as a sofa. There is free deliver on orders of £300 and you can spread your payments over 24 or 36 months.

www.furnituremad.co.uk

This website offers a good range of very reasonably priced traditional-style furniture, including beds and dining suites. They also offer accessories such as bedding and lighting. This is an online shopping site, and has the Which? Web Trader seal. This means the site has been accredited by the UK's Consumer Association, so it is recognised as a good trader site.

The site offers free delivery to any UK address, and there are different discounts and special offers on selected items every month.

www.habitat.net

This is the homepage of the Habitat stores. You cannot actually order online as yet – this is more of an online catalogue. But it shows you the latest range of Habitat's modern, minimalist furniture and home accessories (such as lighting, rugs, vases and storage systems), and is another good source of inspiration.

www.trackuk.force9.co.uk

This website, the homepage of African Trackwoods Ltd, offers something a little bit different. This company specialises in furniture made from recycled wood sourced from naturally weathered Zimbabwean railway sleepers. You therefore have the opportunity to obtain high-quality furniture from a source of exotic hardwood that does not deplete the environment. Every item of furniture is unique, and it is possible to have pieces custom-made. The company also makes artefacts such as desk accessories, picture frames, jewellery boxes and carvings. Be warned though – the prices of these unique items are steep.

GARDENING

These are useful websites to browse when you are looking for plants, equipment, furniture or general inspiration for your garden.

www.gardenlinks.ndo.co.uk

This very comprehensive website is an internet directory for UK gardening and gardens. There are links to hundreds of other related sites, organised into sections such as fruit and vegetables, tools and equipment, shrubs and trees, organic gardening, growing herbs, wildlife, pests and diseases, and furniture and ornaments.

www.greenfingers.com

This website is an online gardening centre. Its departments include plants; tools and equipment; pots, tubs and baskets; chemicals and fertilisers; compost; fencing; decking and patios, garden buildings; lawnmowers and lawncare; and lighting and water features. There also is an inspirational section of planting ideas. There's even a section on topiary made easy, so if you fancy carving your shrubs into animal shapes, this is where to start. You can also email your gardening queries to a professional gardener and have a reply within 48 hours. The site is Which? Web Trader accredited, so online ordering is guaranteed to be safe.

hortic.com

This site, compiled by gardening enthusiasts, contains a plant directory, suggestions for reading, and directories of nurseries, gardening associations and gardening societies.

www.martex.co.uk/hta

This is the website of the Horticultural Trades Association. You can search their comprehensive directories for garden centres, nurseries, landscapers, retailers and wholesalers.

www.rhs.org.uk

The website of the Royal Horticultural Society includes a very useful Plant Finder section. This exists to put gardeners in touch with suppliers of plants. There are more than 70,000 plants in the database, many of them unusual.

GENERAL

The following are general sites for homes and gardens.

www.bbb.co.uk/homes

This is an umbrella site from which you can connect to other BBC home-related sites. They are the homepages for various BBC programmes covering DIY and interior design, and broader topics such as antiques, the property market, personal finance issues and consumer affairs. Not simply an advert for the programmes, the sites include a lot of expert advice, links to other useful sites of interest, and the opportunity to put your queries to an expert. These sites contain a lot of sources of inspiration.

bbc.co.uk/gardening is a similar set-up for gardens. It includes useful information such as what gardening tasks to do at what time of year, a plant directory, and an area on which users share their favourite tips and ideas.

There's even a feature telling you how your sign of the zodiac relates to your gardening style!

www.in-out.dircon.co.uk

This site gives advice on many aspects of home improvements, painting and decorating, and gardening and landscaping. They offer free estimates (in and around Greater London) to receive professional advice. There is also a feature where you can post questions.

INSPIRATION

The following sites are useful to browse if you are seeking ideas and inspiration.

moresplashthancash.com

This website contains some interesting tips for transforming rooms for those on a tight budget.

www.whittakerwoods.com

This is the website for Zoffany, a manufacturer and supplier of high-quality wallpapers, fabrics, paints, trimmings and carpets. Zoffany draws its inspiration from its archive, producing translations and interpretations of documents. With an international colour palette, Zoffany crafts both a traditional timeless look, as well as a more contemporary feel, through its products. Operating in the luxury sector of the interiors industry, Zoffany designs and creates products that are used by leading interior designers and architects. Its fabrics and wallpapers can be seen in many private residences and leading hotels all over the world.

SALVAGE

The following sites are a good starting place if you are looking for reclaimed materials for your renovation.

www.acedemo.co.uk

This is the homepage of ACE Reclamation in Dorset. This is the salvage yard where we bought our staircase – one of my best buys. Their stocks change weekly but include timber, fire inserts and fire surrounds, flagstones, oak and pine panelling, chimney pots, weathered bricks, cast iron column radiators, pavers, cobbles, roll-top baths, Victorian basins, banister spindles, and roof tiles.

www.arcsal.com

Arcsal.com offers an online catalogue of architectural salvage materials. They have a wide range of goods organised into categories such as authentic replicas; doors and gates; bathrooms and kitchens; furniture; church architecture; and radiators and fireplaces. Their stock includes items such as columns, statues, panelling and stained glass. You can order online, or if you are looking for something specific and can't find it in their catalogue, they will look for the item for you through their national network of dealers.

www.demolitions.co.uk

This is the website of Eden Garden Antiques. They specialise in reclaimed materials, including timber and stone. They stock reclaimed solid wood doors, mahogany benches, oak beams, windows, lintels, roundels, flagstones and cobbles. They have a particularly good supply of reclaimed wooden flooring, much of which is Victorian and comes from the demolition of public buildings such as hospitals. Based in Cumbria, they offer delivery anywhere within the UK and also export overseas.

www.ebuild.co.uk

This useful web directory includes contact details for DIY and house renovation suppliers. They are organised into headings such as architectural salvage; bricks and stone; builders' merchants; flooring; green energy; roofing; timber; and wrought iron. They also have a listing for services such as specialist builders; garden design;

architectural services; interior design; and surveying. The site also carries details of self-build events and exhibitions around the UK.

www.fairbank.ltd.uk/theyard

The Yard has an interesting selection of architectural antiques, garden ornaments, and reclaimed building materials. Their goods include reclaimed beams, floorboards and woodblock flooring, fireplaces and radiators. They also have interesting items such as cider presses, cheese presses, pig benches, stone troughs and grindstones.

www.recserv.demon.co.uk

This is the website of Reclamation Services Ltd, dealers in original and bespoke architectural items, garden ornaments and decorative elements. Their extensive stock features Georgian and Victorian chimneypieces and garden features, including stone fountains, entire pavilions and orangeries. They offer the facility to order online.

www.salvoweb.com

This is the website of Westland and Company. They offer a good range of antique, period and decorative chimneypieces, fire grates, and architectural items such as panelling, grills, gates, fountains and plaques. There's no online shopping facility, but you can have a pleasant time browsing.

www.umbrian.com

Umbrian is the largest supplier of old materials for architecture in central Italy, with a selection of beautiful floor tiles, fireplaces, stone and marble window frames, arches, terracotta bricks and fountains. This is a lovely site to browse for inspiration if you are thinking of a Mediterranean theme, and if your budget can stretch to some 16th-century statues, the company can ship their goods anywhere in the world.

STORAGE

The following website offers some good solutions for storage facilities.

www.cotswoldco.com

This company specialises in value-for-money storage ideas and accessories. Their site is conveniently arranged by room, such as home office, living room, bedroom, bathroom and kitchen. Clutter is a problem for many of us, and this company has some innovative ideas for CD racks, TV cabinets, shelving units, bathroom cabinets, magazine holders, kitchen organisers and home office equipment.

TOOLS

The following sites offer all the tools you will ever need to complete your renovation work.

www.axminster.co.uk

This site offers an offline shopping option if you are wary about performing your transaction online. There are very useful, detailed descriptions of all tools and products, their use and care.

www.cooksons.co.uk

This site carries detailed descriptions of more than 50,000 products, often discounted from the recommended retail price. This site also is Which? Web Trader accredited.

www.directtoolsales.co.uk

This website offers good deals on popular brands such as DeWalt and Bosch. This site has the Which? Web Trader certificate.

www.diytools.co.uk

This site features a good range of tools at competitive prices. There is free UK delivery on orders over £50.

Index

Design Revolution would like to thank Andrew Easton for producing the plans of the house and the garden; Richard Wheatley for reference photography; and Tony Hodgson for sound advice at the eleventh hour.